LAUNCH YOUR OWN
MAGAZINE

LAUNCH YOUR OWN
MAGAZINE

A GUIDE FOR SUCCEEDING IN TODAY'S MARKETPLACE

Samir A. Husni, Ph.D.

Mr. Magazine™

Hamblett House Inc.

Nashville, Tennessee

Interviews were edited for clarity and style.

Publisher: Hamblett House Inc., 4117 Hillsboro Road, Suite 103322,
Nashville, TN 37215.
Distributor: Oxbridge Communications Inc.
150 Fifth Avenue, Suite 302, New York, NY 10011
Telephone: 1-800/955-0231, 212/741-0231
Facsimile: 212/633-2938
URL: http://www.mediafinder.com

Library of Congress Catalog Card Number: 98-85707

ISBN: 0-9661049-0-0

99 98   3 2 1

Printed in the United States of America

Cover design: Bruce Gore, Gore Studio Inc.
Cover photographer: Robert Jordan
Printer: Victor Graphics Inc.

Contents

This work is dedicated to my loving children—
Diala, Laura, and Afeef.

Thanks go to the Department of Journalism,
University of Mississippi, for allowing me the time
to work on this book;

my assistants, Roger C. "Trey" Alberson III,
Andrew T. Burns, and Jane Dorsett;

the magazine professionals who shared their
time and talent within these pages;

Amy Lyles Wilson, my publisher,
friend, and former student;

and, as always, my wife, Marie.

Introduction

One of the first things I was told after coming to America from Lebanon was that whenever two or three Americans get together, the first thing they want to do is form a committee. The second thing they want to do is start a publication for that committee.

That was twenty years ago, and times have changed. Now, you start the publication first, then form the committee. Thus, America is witnessing (and reading) a boom in the magazine industry. Never before have so many people launched so many magazines in so little time. In 1985, just over 200 magazines were launched. By 1997, the number had quadrupled, to 852!

With this explosion in mind, the magazine entrepreneurs of the future can look to this book as a starting point for their ventures. The idea behind this book, though, started back in my middle-school years when I would sit in geometry class and daydream about launching my own magazine. I would borrow the circles, squares, and rhombuses so that I could doodle renditions of magazine covers in my notepad.

I soon realized that launching a magazine, whether you use a compass and protractor or a Power Mac, is a creative piece of work that cannot be pinned down to a single, easily memorizable formula. However, after publishing *Samir Husni's Guide to New Consumer Magazines* for more than twelve years, and after working and consulting on numerous magazine projects, I felt the need for some kind of guidebook—a starting point that would increase the pleasure quotient in publishing, while minimizing the headaches and pitfalls. I want this book to be a launching pad for people who are pursuing their dreams.

I felt the best format for illustrating the creative ways to launch a magazine was to include interviews with some of the publishers and editors who have come before you. You'll get a fly-on-the-wall perspective of what it takes to get a magazine off the ground. Although each tale is different, each one reinforces the ideas I've written about and should contribute a great deal to your knowledge of the industry.

So, without further adieu, let's begin your journey to the top of the staff box!

Samir A. Husni

First things first. Before diving headlong into the guts of the magazine launch business, we need to understand the nature of the beast we're creating.

WHAT *IS* A MAGAZINE?

1

The magazine is a nebulous medium. It defies concise definitions, wriggling in and out of other media playgrounds. It informs, entertains, and, above all, interacts with the "audience of one." No other format delivers a more powerful, one-two punch of graphic design and creative writing. And no other medium is harder to pigeonhole.

In this age of technological wizardry, magazines defy logic. They thrive without embedded microchips or satellite feeds, yet manage to bring us closer together.

But what are they?

SEMANTICS

The word has been around much longer than the medium. *Magazine* has traditionally meant "a storehouse," whether in French (*magasin*), Italian (*magassino*), or Arabic (*makaszan*). Though the word started as a description for a silo or a warehouse, the term has evolved into that dangerous little clip slid into the handle of a 9mm Smith & Wesson. Since 1721, it has been used to describe our main course here: the periodical publication.

However, to say a magazine is a "storehouse of information" may be misleading. A newspaper is also a storehouse of information, as is a newsletter, a college yearbook, a Web page, and so on. Even such television programs as *20/20* and *Dateline NBC* call themselves magazines. In this day and age, where information is the supreme commodity, we need to differentiate between what a magazine is and what a magazine is not.

The two major definitions for magazines come from the good old days.

First, we have the patriarch of the study of magazines, Frank Luther Mott. He authored the five-volume set, *A History of American Magazines*, and founded the Missouri School of Journalism. Mott was the first one to give us a working definition that everyone could agree on, and its four basic tenets hold true to this day.

1. Periodical

A magazine must have a preexisting, periodical frequency that can be relied on.

2. Bound

There must be some kind of staple, glue, or thread that binds the magazine.

3. Varied

In the good old days, newspapers contained nothing but news. Magazines, then, came as a cure for slow news days with their witty, interesting features on a variety of topics.

4. Printed

Don't laugh. These things need to be pointed out. This particular criterion was crafted at a time when "must be printed" meant a magazine could not be handwritten. There was no mention of the Internet, of radio, or of television. We're talking *old*.

THE POST OFFICE

We don't stop with Mott on our quest for a working definition. Apparently, definitions are like opinions—everybody's got one—and there's a vested interest involved in their formation.

We come a little closer to the final product when we combine the above criteria with what Benjamin Franklin set up in the eighteenth century when he was Postmaster General. Franklin treated the magazine industry well. He set up the different classes we still use to send letters and packages through the mail. He invented this structure as a gimmick to help along the newspapers and magazines of his time. Under his system, surplus revenue from first-class postage (letters) and third-class postage (junk mail) helped fund the second-class postage deficit incurred by the inexpensive mailing of subscription based magazines and newspapers.

Until recently, *Time* magazine could be sent second-class for 31¢. At first-class rates, it would cost nearly $3!

A few years ago, second-class rates skyrocketed nearly 500% when Congress declared that each class of postage must pay for itself. No more free meals for second-class. But don't fret, because second-class is still significantly cheaper than first-class.

A few years ago, the second-class rates skyrocketed nearly 500% when Congress declared that each class of postage must pay for itself.

Now, the post office is not without its own definition of what makes a magazine a magazine. Its primary requirement is that the publication be printed no fewer than four times per year. Anything not printed four times per year gets dropped to third-class, with its motley crew of junk mail and throwaways.

MY TWO CENTS' WORTH

I'd like to throw my own requirement into the mix: a magazine must be able to be touched. We're hip deep in media today. We've got television, radio, and the Internet providing us with a great deal of information currently available in magazines. However, you can't fold a radio, work a crossword puzzle on TV, or surf the Net on the subway (without getting mugged, that is).

Magazines rule over all other competing media in terms of portability, ease of use, and cost. Magazines lord the sense of touch over their foes with grace and creativity. They achieve a supremely personal, interactive relationship with their readers, delivering the most information possible in the cheapest package available.

So what happens to publications like *Victoria*, that test one issue on the newsstands and don't put out a second issue for another six months? The post office may not recognize that as a magazine. So what do we call it? It looks, it reads, and it feels just like a magazine, but because some faceless entity decided "four times per year" is the postal mantra, then it doesn't qualify officially.

Oh, What a Tangled Web

To me, anything that hits the market and is available to the general public is a magazine. Whether it folds out and becomes a big poster or whether it's a CD-ROM that can be printed out and stapled, it's still a magazine. Web pages, on the other hand, are not magazines. They are Web pages. They may be a storehouse of information, but they are far from achieving magazinehood primarily because they could never be on the newsstand, in the mailbox, or on the coffee table. You cannot scan a magazine rack and have your eyes hit *Esquire*, then *Glamour*, then www.salonmag.com.

> **Magazines rule over all other competing media in terms of portability, ease of use, and cost.**

Slate, Microsoft's venture, eventually became a *real* magazine when the company realized that dedicating yourself exclusively to the Internet does not make sense financially. Expect others to do the same thing. Web magazines are not long for this world—cyber or otherwise.

SPLIT PERSONALITY

As strict as these requirements are, two main varieties of magazines do exist—consumer and trade.

Consumer Magazines

Consumer magazines are those available to the general public that can be purchased anywhere magazines are sold. Whether you're at a grocery store, a bookstore, or a sidewalk newsstand in New York City, whether it's *TV Guide*, *Esquire*, or *Raygun*, every magazine on the shelf is a consumer magazine. In 1997, there were 5,200 consumer magazines available in the United States. By contrast, in 1980, there were only 2,000.

Trade Magazines

On the other hand, we have trade, or "business to business" magazines. These publications are aimed at a specific profession and are sent directly to that audience. Whether it's *Ad Age* for the advertising industry, *Beef Week* for the cattle industry, or *Nails* for folks who work in salons, they're all microniched periodicals geared toward a specific business. Today, there are approximately 12,000 trade magazines in America—nearly triple the number of consumer publications!

Other

In addition to both the trade and consumer magazine industries, we have such publications as religious magazines, which are not readily available to anyone outside a given organization. For instance, *Catholic Digest* is not on newsstands, nor is it geared toward a specific profession.

THE LOGICAL CONCLUSION

There are approximately 21,000 magazine titles available in America today.

Add together all of these various types of publications and the number reaches around 21,000 magazine titles available in America today. As you might suppose, they pretty much cover every subject imaginable.

So you want to start a magazine? Well, I suggest you come up with something entirely different. If your topic of choice has already been covered, make sure your treatment is different, original.

That's the key.

NOTES

....
....
....
....
....
....
....
....
....
....
....
....
....
....
....
....
....
....

The United States magazine market is witnessing one of the greatest explosions in terms of the number of new magazine launches.

MARKET OVERVIEW

2

In March 1998 alone, 121 new magazine titles were launched. Both the effects of new technologies, such as personal computers and presses that cater to small publishers, and the demand for more information in less time and less space gave the magazine industry a fertile ground for more launches.

Since 1985, the number of new consumer magazines arriving at the marketplace has steadily increased.

The number of titles distributed to the nation's newsstands or made available to the general public increased from 3,000 in 1990 to 5,200 in 1997.

STAYING ALIVE

However, it should be noted that among those magazines launched in 1995 and whose intended frequency was four times annually, approximately 53% are now dead. And only approximately 28% of the magazines launched in 1991 were still in business after four years of publishing. Thus, it is safe to say that at the four-year mark, the survival rate of magazines published with an intended frequency of four times or higher has been 30%. This number illustrates a big increase from the 1985 magazine survival rates. At that time, only 18.9% of new magazines (or two out of ten) would remain in business after four years.

The most crucial time is the first year. Approximately 73% of the magazines that cease publication within the first year do so after no more than two issues. The rest struggle through a third or maybe fourth issue. Therefore, statistically speaking, if you survive your first four issues, you increase dramatically your chances of staying alive.

Approximately 73% of the magazines that cease publication within the first year do so after no more than two issues.

Turning a Profit

Of course, staying alive is different from turning a profit. Based on research and other consulting projects I have witnessed or conducted, the average profitability schedule is as such: The larger the magazine (in terms of circulation and frequency), the more losses to expect in the first three years. The goal is to break even in four years, making the fifth year the time to start showing profits.

Publishing a magazine is a long-range investment. Magazines that choose a weekly or monthly frequency and a circulation of more than half a million are expected to lose money and show no profit in the early years. However, I am quick to add that those same magazines, if they survive the initial few years, become the cash cows for their companies. Yes, it costs more to produce a monthly or a weekly, and, yes, the odds are against you in the beginning. But all my data show that once you turn the corner, barring unforeseen circumstances, the magazine will generate profits and remain in the black.

Selling Out

As the magazine continues to publish, it will simultaneously be establishing a cash value in which investors are interested. The rate for which an established magazine is purchased is now between ten to twelve times its gross revenue. Recently, though, the sale of a major West Coast magazine company reportedly fetched approximately twenty times the company's gross revenue. Investors should expect to break even after four years and then enjoy a steady increase in the return of their investments. I might add that there have been few, and I emphasize *few*, magazines that were able to break even within the first

The rate for which an established magazine is purchased is now between ten to twelve times its gross revenue.

year and make a profit in the second year. But none of them were published on a monthly or weekly basis.

REVENUE OVERVIEW

Consumer magazines depend on two major sources of revenue: circulation and advertising. Although the current data show that established magazines are at a stage where circulation revenues account for approximately 52% of their income and advertising revenues carry the remaining 48%, new magazines bring in 83% of their revenues from circulation and 17% from advertising.

Circulation

There is no doubt that we are in a circulation-driven era of magazine publishing. Although a major country music magazine was able to reach the one-million circulation mark and was named the fastest growing magazine in terms of circulation, it remains far behind the number of ad pages that you would expect to see in such a publication. Advertisers are weary of new magazines, first because of their numbers and second because of the unpredictability of their survival.

Therefore, magazine publishers are investing more money and efforts in the establishment of a solid circulation base for any new publication. One of the three largest magazine companies in this country plans all of its launches to reach the 750,000 circulation mark within four years. If those projections are not met, the magazine project is killed.

More Mags, Lower Numbers

Though the number of new magazines is on the rise, the big circulation numbers are not following suit. The average circulation of new magazines is approximately 70,000—a low figure when compared to established magazines, yet high when compared to the number of new, specialized magazines that may tout a circulation of 10,000 and 15,000. Somehow, 100,000 has become the magic number that gets the ear of national advertisers. However, it does not guarantee their business.

The average circulation of new magazines is approximately 70,000.

Thus, with the help of twenty or so independent national distributors, those new magazines are being launched with low circulation figures and high cover prices in hopes of surviving based on magazine sales. The average cover price for a new magazine is approaching $5.00, whereas established publications run about $2.50.

The average cover price for a new magazine is approaching $5.00, whereas established publications run about $2.50.

New magazine plans, on average, call for an initial national circulation of 70,000—strictly based on single-copy sales for the first year. The second year's projected goal is to double this number through a mix of subscription and single-copy sales. By year four, circulation should be at 250,000.

Advertising

In terms of advertising pages, new magazines have not exceeded 19% of publications of 92 total pages. Since 1990, advertising has accounted for, on average, 17 pages in 92-page magazines. However, during the same period, some magazines broke advertising page records en route to bankruptcy. The consumer magazine record holder is *PC Sources*, a magazine published by Ziff-Davis. In 1990, it carried 417 ad pages in its premiere issue. The magazine died three years later.

Since 1990, advertising has accounted for, on average, 17 pages in 92-page magazines.

Ad/ed ratio

New magazines plan for a 20/80 ad/ed ratio in their first year, 25/75 ad/ed ratio in their second year, 30/70 ad/ed ratio in their third year, and 40/60 ad/ed ratio in their fourth year. However, the first year's ratio has never been a good indicator of the second or third years. So many variables play a significant role in the first year of the magazine that, regardless of the first year's results, the second and third years can easily go above or below the projected plan. In terms of ad revenues, the charter year, so far, has not been a good indicator of what is in store for the future. However, surviving the charter year is a good indicator of your chances of staying alive.

INFINITE VARIABLES

I wish there were some kind of a litmus test that could

forecast the future of a magazine, or some kind of formula that one could follow. This is, first and foremost, a creative product that is affected by an infinite number of variables. Any one change in any one variable can alter the course of the magazine.

Early in 1996, skyrocketing paper costs brought the number of new launches to a halt. In July of that same year, paper costs dropped and new magazine launches exploded.

Magazines that depend on direct mail for their survival are at the mercy of the post office. Any change in mailing expenses can mean a great deal to a magazine.

Magazines are dependent products and thus they cannot be treated as independent variables when analyzing their prospects of survival.

Take your best shot.

NOTES

. . . .

. . . .

. . . .

. . . .

. . . .

. . . .

. . . .

. . . .

. . . .

. . . .

. . . .

. . . .

. . . .

. . . .

. . . .

. . . .

Susan Thompson is the CEO and president of New South Publishing Inc. in Atlanta, Georgia. She founded Know Atlanta *magazine, the premier relocation guide to the city of Atlanta, in 1986.*

Interview:

Susan Thompson
Know Atlanta

How did you come up with the idea for *Know Atlanta*?

I had been in the advertising business for twelve years. I had kids, so in order to have time for my family, I would try to work for some lower profile advertising agencies. But I found myself in a real dilemma concerning just how much time I wanted to spend.

At that point, my sister and her husband were offered a move to California. He was going to a market that would have given them the raise. She got the big bonus, and he got the big increase in salary with all the perks and bells and whistles. She was asked to come out to California and start her big house-hunting trip.

As she prepared for her trip, she looked at the varying costs of living in Atlanta as compared to L.A. She was convinced that with $600,000 there in a house, she felt she would be able to pick out anything she wanted to match the quality of life she was accustomed to. Her husband had moved some weeks earlier, and he was already settled in and was beginning to get acclimated to his job. Well, she flies out there and is picked up in a Jag and given a tour of the hills of L.A.

It turns out that this $600,000 house that she thought was

a very nice house turned out to be a three-bed, two-bath, with its second roof and third furnace. Well, she had been in real estate for years prior to that, so rather than just get totally frustrated, she continued to shop around.

What was supposed to be a two- or three-day trip to L.A. became almost a three-week trip, and she took it upon herself to become the diligent student of the L.A. lifestyle. Three and a half weeks later, she was looking at $3½ million homes in Santa Barbara.

She couldn't afford a $3½ million home in Santa Barbara, so she packed up her bags and came back to Atlanta. We were sitting around one day having coffee, and I was absolutely frustrated with trying to juggle the crazy world of advertising with family.

We are both crying over our beer about our lot in life, and she looks across the table at me and says, "You know, Susan, if all the people moving to Atlanta are as frustrated as I just was in beginning my search for a home in L.A., then maybe you should do some kind of newcomer lifestyle magazine." From the context of a real estate agent who found herself on the other side of the table, it just made all sorts of sense to us. What was to be an hour coffee became almost an all-night vigil about the dilemma of the transferring employee and the dynamics of the impact of the move on families.

What did you do to move from this brainstorming phase to an actual magazine launch mindset?

I made the decision to go to people who were smarter than I. I have always had that philosophy—if you want to learn about a new idea or a new way of doing things, you don't have to reinvent the wheel. You just have to go to people who have been in that business. The only publishing people I knew were a couple of gentlemen who owned a printing company on the south side of town.

I went to see them, told them about my idea, and basically got in the trenches with them. They put me in a warehouse behind the shipping department of this printing company. Actually, they had been printing an apartment magazine for a couple of years, and it had been a miserable failure. They really did not know what they wanted. They had printed an apartment magazine for a woman, and she had not been able to pay her bills. They decided, "Well, if she is really out of business before she ever got in business, then maybe we should put her back in and see if she can't get this thing off the ground." I think she lasted less than a year. When I walked in there was just this skeleton of what was left of the publication.

We sat down and we discussed it for weeks, maybe even six months, as to the direction we wanted. I also kept relying on my sister, since she was a real estate agent and had experienced the misery of relocation firsthand. We kept bringing her in, and she brought in other agents for their input and ideas about whether we were on track.

We went about the task of figuring out how to get writing teams together to handle this subject. The beauty of this magazine is that it is not investigative journalism. Every story is about "how to"—how to get a doctor, how to buy a home or your first home, how to place your children in a public or private school, which schools we endorse, so it wasn't brain surgery.

In talking to human resource directors and some of Atlanta's top companies and the CEOs of companies who had recently moved into the city, we heard some very similar stories. All had experienced all sorts of problems when they brought new people in. Commercial brokers, especially. They're on the front lines every day meeting with customers, be it an individual who might rent 1,500 square feet and hire a secretary locally, or the president of UPS, such as when that company moved its worldwide headquarters here. They all have very basic, similar needs, and those needs became the editorial calendar for the magazine.

We started out as a semi-annual, only because we didn't know any better. We knew that we didn't want to be an annual, because we realized that people would forget about us if we only sold once a year. We thought a six-month selling cycle would give us every chance to sell as much of the book as possible.

How did you fund it?

I was lucky that I had a husband who had a salary, so I didn't really need a big salary. We gave ourselves $12,000. I didn't have any problem expensing the warehouse. I mean this thing was so grimy. I was in an old warehouse room, and behind me was a syrup factory that made syrup for snowcones. The place was just infested with rats. I never saw any, but I heard them all the time. And the factory's production ran like clockwork—Monday was banana, Tuesday was strawberry, Wednesday was grape—and the smell was overpowering.

But it didn't bother me at all. I was so excited and so high on the concept. There was such a worthiness. I felt very noble with my idea of helping the tens of thousands of families who were moving into Atlanta. I kept bringing my sister back in, and she served as an adviser for a long time.

How did you handle design?

Having worked in advertising for as long as I did, all I had to do was go to some of my designer friends and ask if they would be interested in designing a magazine. Not one of Atlanta's top designers turned me down. I offered them next to nothing, but they all wanted to do it. What I didn't realize was that designers love to do what they have never done before.

These designers were typically coming out of ad agencies from around the city and had done every kind of ad. They had done every brochure and created every thirty- or sixty-second spot imaginable, but no one had ever given them the opportunity to work on a magazine.

On a shoestring budget, Atlanta's top designer, Don Trousdel, designed *Know* for us. He just put his best art on the cover. Don is the type that just breathes and wins—he is that good. The first cover won the Art Directors of New York Award. It was a motif of people sort of flying around on the page carrying peaches.

I knew enough from my years in advertising to know that even the smallest award or the smallest kind word from an advertiser should be publicized. That much I knew. The testimonial letters that we received came in fast and furiously, and they were used. The awards that we were getting for the cover and design were then reintegrated into the selling effort.

Soon enough, we found ourselves in business with our first issue in April 1986. Well, we head out the door—we being me and one other person—and we start selling for the October 1987 issue. We publicized the book, and we printed 25,000 twice a year. With the first issue in April, we had a good circulation. We got them all out, but we didn't have a lot of people requesting more magazines. But we felt like we were doing well because of healthy advertising.

We published the October issue, which was supposed to be available until April 1988. Six weeks after it goes out, we are totally out of magazines. I go to my mentor, Jack Moran, whom I had met through the course of all of this. He had been helping us along the way to make good decisions. Mentors mean everything in this business. They are usually people who have been there and done that, and they can really help guide you.

We go to lunch, and I am literally in tears. I say, "What am I going to do? I have this magazine that I have charged people $3,000 a page for, and I have promised these people that this thing is going to be around until next April—and here I am out of magazines." I will never forget—he just threw his head back and just laughed. He said, "My dear, you have the problem that publishers pray for. Don't you understand that you have more demand than you have magazines? You must go quarterly in January."

But I said, "Jack, I can't go quarterly in January. Here it is November. How in the world am I going to sell people?" He said, "Give them a discount for January, and then go quarterly."

In our gut we knew we had something outrageous. We bit the big bullet, made our announcement, and just had an unbelievable demand for the news that we were going quarterly. I maintained 85% of my ad base. I literally doubled people's ad-dollar commitment to us.

How did you continue to attract advertisers?

Oh, that's easy—the key issues affecting a transferee are the key advertising prospects. And I can say that about all magazines. The key people affecting the industry are the buyers and service providers. In the case of *Know Atlanta*, it was private schools, hospitals, apartments, physicians, mortgagees, and so forth. We took them right down that yellow brick road of buying a home or apartment, getting a mortgage or a bank, moving children into a public or private school, all of that.

All the other magazines that we publish today have those key factors. Take, for example, our magazine called *Net News*, which is for the official Atlanta Lawn Tennis Association. We've got Nike and Adidas, K-Swiss, Converse. We go to the industries that feed tennis players.

Let's go back to the point where you went quarterly with *Know Atlanta*.

As I mentioned, we discounted that January issue, and then we went to 100,000. We benefitted because the city of Atlanta was also enjoying a tremendous amount of publicity from being chosen the number-one city in the country in which to own a business. It was also the number-one city in terms of economic development.

The city itself was really in hot pursuit of corporate relocation, and that was the pulse we felt when we started the magazine. My sister, the realtor, already knew this because of all the corporate transferees who were showing up on her doorstep needing a home. And the advertising prospects were hearing it as I walked in the door. So we knew that it would work.

We went quarterly in January 1988, and we have been quarterly ever since. We now have a circulation of 162,000. We stayed quarterly, but we increased the circulation for each issue.

How did you grow into more publications?

I decided I wanted to take *Know* into other cities. If it could work in Atlanta, it darn well could work in any other city experiencing the kind of growth we have here. For instance, Las Vegas is the biggest market today. It's Atlanta on the East Coast, and Las Vegas on the West.

At the time, Tampa was getting a lot of attention. I went to my two partners in the printing company and said, "Let's start the expansion of *Know*." They asked me how long it took to get *Know Atlanta* really healthy, so we looked back over our history books, and we could see that it really took about three years. We thought, "Gosh, how are we going to fund another magazine? Right now we have one magazine that pays for all the lights and water and gas and car expenses. How are we going to use that one title to fund another?"

We had to make a decision: go into our own pocketbooks to fund the expansion or seek a new revenue source.

We had been hearing about custom publishing. We had actually been approached a couple of times about doing custom pieces, so we investigated a few opportunities. We were just getting comfortable with this whole process when the Atlanta Lawn Tennis Association, which is the world's largest organized tennis association, came about.

We were all members of the association, and we knew they had been doing a newspaper for seventeen years. The people behind it were of the typical newspaper mentality. The feature articles were all done at the same time that the late-breaking news was written. We explained to them that that really isn't how it needs to be done. We could do feature articles earlier, and we could develop an editorial calendar. We could then do departments, and then the late-breaking stats of the players and teams could be done at the last minute. That way, we would be able to put the magazine together very quickly.

They loved that. They gave us the contract, and we have had it for six years. And we loved it, too. There was no question about the circulation—that is the beauty of customer pieces and of organizational magazines. We already had the ad committal game down, and we knew who we were as a publishing firm.

It was a brilliant success. Tennis was hot. Advertisers like Wilson and Nike were ready to place their ads in a magazine format that was actually an oversized newspaper. They just came in droves.

It had wonderful profit margins, so we started feeding those profits back into the expansion of *Know*. We took it into Tampa about three years ago, and Denver a year-and-a-half ago. Now we have eight magazines in our contract division, and it just keeps getting richer and richer. Our goal is to take *Know* into a new market about every three years.

Is there anything you would have done differently?

I think I would learn management skills a lot earlier. When you are an entrepreneur with a strong vision, you'll head out the door assuming everyone is with you. You assume that, based on the few conversations you have with your sales reps and coworkers, that everyone in your office is right there with you. The horror comes when you stop and look to your left and you look to your right and realize there is no one there. The fact is, they never did follow you because you never told them how to do it.

There were two or three sales reps who came to me early in the game. Today, I would give my right arm to have them back. They were the best, and I was too stupid and too unsophisticated to keep them on the team. So the one thing that I didn't do was get that management training so I could bring the team together. Am I a good manager now? Well, I am a better manager. I have learned to listen, and I have learned to build a group vision.

Besides managerial skills, is there anything else you would have changed early in the project?

The way that I regarded my family. It takes a tremendous toll on the family. I have been very fortunate, because my mother has helped out a lot. But all too often, I did put family second.

But it's a love affair. I always say that I have three children—two kids and *Know*. I think that I could probably have done a better job at balancing all of that, but it's really difficult. I have great children and a wonderful family, but along the way, I could have done things differently.

What advice would you give to someone with a great idea for a magazine?

I've actually had this happen many times. I just have this great desire to share this joy and to share this blessing. When people come to me with their ideas, rather than my saying, "I learned this my way, the hard way—you go do this yourself," I will always set an appointment with them, and I will always meet with them.

Too often, I see the sketchiness in the back of their eyes. I see the unwillingness to reach, to be all they are capable of being. And then every so often I see that spark, and I say, "That one is going to make it."

NOTES

· ·

· ·

· ·

· ·

· ·

· ·

· ·

· ·

· ·

· ·

· ·

· ·

· ·

· ·

· ·

· ·

· ·

If you're going to spend the rest of your professional life with your magazine, you had better love it. I don't mean a sweet, romantic love. I mean, you need to have a torrid, passionate love affair with your subject matter. You must consume it and be consumed by it. Both you and your magazine must have the energy to stay fresh for the long haul.

THE CONCEPT

3

Not long ago, I consulted on the launch of *Longbows & Recurves* magazine. Before it hit the newsstands, the publisher was in my office with the sheets from the first issue in his lap. Nothing had been stapled; his baby had just rolled off the presses. On one hand he was terrified, and on the other, obviously, he was on cloud nine. This was as close to childbirth as he was ever going to get, and he was savoring the moment.

BUT NOT FOR ME

Now, I tried to stir the same passion in myself that he was spilling all over my office. No such luck. The subject matter of this publication was so foreign to me that if I were the one in charge, I would have folded up shop on the first day.

I don't go bow hunting. I've never had an intimate relationship with a handgun. I've never killed anything bigger than a spider. But this is *his* life. He's taken his kids hunting since they were knee-high to a shotgun shell. Hunting animals for sport is a part of his life.

Needless to say, he was proud. I had e-mailed him earlier in the day and told him to read every page, every word, to get a unified perspective of his creation. After he had done so, there he sat, beaming—right there in my office.

I took the pages from him and flipped through them myself. I was tempted to read the article on raccoon hunting, but thought, well, maybe some other time. I'm sure it would be fun if I shared his interest. Good thing I was just the consultant.

This example provides perhaps the most important, most cram-it-in-your-head-and-keep-it-there point of all. That is, if this editor and publisher conducts his editorial office the way it should be conducted, I will never be interested in reading his magazine.

THE CONSTANT CONCEPT

Here's why: The concept is the only constant.

Did you get that? Read it again. Memorize it. Etch it into your Mac keyboard. Everything else may change at your magazine: you'll hire and fire editors; you'll upgrade technology; you'll freshen up your graphic design; you'll increase advertising revenue as a percentage of gross profits. But your concept will remain constant.

Your concept is your guideline, your mission statement. Lose sight of it and you're dead.

Think of it like this: Your magazine's editorial concept is like a lighthouse on the foggy coastline. It's always there. All incoming ships look to it for direction. Same thing with your editorial content. The concept is your guideline, your mission statement. Everything that ends up in your baby must look to this lighthouse of a concept for direction. Take your eyes off of it for one second and you hit the rocks.

Be Brief

Your concept may be the most difficult copy you'll ever write because it has to be a paragraph of no more than two or three sentences. For those of you who like to write, you know this is brain surgery. You have to condense the life of a magazine that could conceivably span fifty or one hundred years into one little paragraph. It must plainly state what the magazine is going to be about, whom it will reach, and who will be advertising in it.

IT'S A BUSINESS

Before we burrow too deeply into the editorial concept of your magazine, I need to remind you of something: Your magazine is a business. You have a product on your hands that cost you money to produce, and you need to unload it to make a tidy profit. The problem is, magazines are different from any other business. They must be sold not once, but twice: first to the readers, then to the advertisers.

In most cases, you will not be selling a magazine that already exists in reality. Instead, you'll be hawking the concept of a magazine that lives only in your heart and mind. This is why you should be able to recite and discuss your mission at the drop of a hat.

If I ask your name, you don't say, "Uh, well, I think it's Bob." Of course not. I ask your name, and you say, "Bob. My name is Bob." If I want to know your concept, you should rattle it off in less than a minute.

Make It Fit

Why is this important? Because of the lighthouse. Because if you know your guiding light backwards and forwards, you stand a much greater chance of staying on course. Head in one direction. Compare every single article in the magazine to your mission statement and ask yourself if it fits. If it doesn't, drop it like a dead raccoon.

Repeat after me: "My magazine is a business. My magazine is a business." Don't let yourself forget it.

This is why I never want to be tempted to read *Longbows & Recurves*. If *I'm* interested in one of this magazine's articles, the publisher is sailing on choppy waters.

DEVELOPING THE CONCEPT

Where do you get your concept? Where do you get ideas? The answer: It doesn't matter.

You could be asleep and bolt upright in bed with an idea for a magazine on iguanas eating cats. You can get ideas from reading other magazines, from watching brain-mush sitcoms, or from conversations with friends. Ask questions, get involved, talk about everything. You get ideas from life.

1. Move Right Along

How can you move coffee shop dialogue to the formal idea stage? At the very least, you must be enterprising and have a passion for magazines. You have to be creative. You cannot launch a magazine if you cannot mold what you see and hear into workable ideas. You have to be able to make things happen.

You are watchdog over your little corner of contemporary culture. Your ideas are the bark, growl, and bite that alert people to your concept.

Magazines reflect society more than any other medium. Therefore, you are watchdog over your little corner of contemporary culture. Your ideas are the bark, growl, and bite that alert people to your concept.

Thus, the development of substantial ideas is the first step toward establishing your concept. Remember, four-year-olds have ideas, too. The act of conceiving is not enough. You must set yourself apart by the creative way you execute your idea.

2. Learn to Share

The second step in the development of your concept is sharing your ideas with friends and relatives. Let them shoot it down if they can. You need that. If you can come up with only one whopping feature story or concept, then you do not belong in this business.

Welcome Opposition

I had a student once who developed an original cooking magazine called, simply, *Grill*. It was all about grilling out on the patio. By the end of the semester, another magazine with the same concept (*On the Grill*) hit the newsstands. Of course, the student was disheartened. But he learned a valuable lesson: Don't throw your arms up in disgust— look for an angle on how your magazine will be different.

It is easier to start a magazine when you have competition than it is to start a magazine without competition. It can unify you and your staff against a common enemy and force you to clarify your concept even further. Don't be afraid to share your ideas. Welcome opposition.

3. Identify the Audience

The third step in developing your concept is identifying your audience. No big deal. All you have to say at this stage of the game is that you think everybody between the ages of 45 and 88 will be interested in your new magazine *How to Be Fit after 55*. Your audience must be at the forefront of your mind when you're hashing out ideas. But remember that the audience is just one of the two groups you must sell your product to.

4. Consider Others

The fourth step in concept development is determining who else on this planet wants to reach those potential readers. You want to speak to them because they will not only purchase advertisements in your magazine, but they will also be dedicated readers.

5. Question Yourself

The fifth, and possibly most bubble-bursting, step is to ask yourself why nobody has dreamed up such a magazine before you. You're dead wrong if you think it's because you're an editor of unparalleled genius.

Don't make the mistake of thinking you're brilliant just because nothing else like it exists. It may have existed before you came onto the scene and have been found to be unprofitable or undoable.

Look at *Prison Life* magazine. When it first came out, the word on the street was, hey, captive audience—can't lose. But who is dying to read about prison life? "I'm going to commit a crime next week, but first, let me read about life in prison. If it sounds good, I'll go commit the crime." The publisher produced two issues before deciding it wasn't working, so it was retooled for people already in prison.

The magazine has one great thing going for it—the audience isn't going anywhere. If they *get* the magazine, they will read the magazine.

Consider the case of *Triumph* magazine a few years back. One of my students dreamed up this magazine for the active handicapped. That is, her primary readership would be people who have disabilities but still function in all capacities of life.

She won first place in the National Student Magazine Competition and the Meredith Corporation, publisher of such magazines as *Better Homes and Gardens* and *Wood*, wanted to launch her idea. However, once Meredith started to research the demographics, the publishers discovered it was nearly impossible to locate the readership. They functioned in society and didn't want to single themselves out. They probably wouldn't pick this magazine off the newsstands, and they almost certainly would not allow their names to be rented for marketing purposes. How can you publish a magazine for a readership you cannot find or have never met?

The first question you must ask yourself about your concept is whether it's an idea for a magazine or an idea for a book.

See? Great idea, but impractical.

Same thing happened with *Grandparent* magazine. A publisher purchased the creator's idea and put it on newsstands. It was a disaster. Sure, everybody loves being a grandparent. But do they need a magazine to affirm it? What are you going to talk about? How to spoil a child? How many cookies are enough? No. After two issues and no response from the audience, it died. Again, it was a good idea that was proven undoable.

Is It a Book?

This leads into my final point for this chapter. The first question you must ask yourself about your concept is whether it's an idea for a magazine or an idea for a book.

Life Cycles

Magazines are different from books in that they have a life cycle. Every week, every month, or every two months, you are putting out a wholly revised publication about the same general stuff. To maintain this, your idea must be able to stand the test of time. If it's a book idea, you write it once and, boom, it's done. Magazines must be born again and again and again.

Content Generation

So how much life is in your idea? How far can you take it? Five years? Ten years? Fifty years? Start thinking about articles. What will you write about in the first issue? What about the second issue? Issue three? If you feel you're running out of steam early in the process, chances are you have a book on your hands. Or, even worse, a flawed concept for a magazine.

IS IT A FAD?

Twelve issues every year may be a lot more than you think. That's why nobody in his right mind launches a magazine today hoping to match the likes of *Good Housekeeping, Better Homes and Gardens, Ladies' Home Journal, Time, Newsweek*—all those established magazines that have become American institutions. Who launches a magazine with a lifespan of one hundred years in mind?

If you start a magazine, your subject matter may go out of style in five or ten years. If so, drop it and launch another one. Even the big dogs are doing that nowadays.

Do you think *Victoria* magazine will be with us in thirty years? Doubtful. We may see an Elizabethan magazine when women tire of the Victorian resurgence, though. Do you think magazines aimed at Windows 95 users will be around when Bill Gates drops the operating system? Of course not. How many Windows 3.1 magazines do you see?

When I say your magazine needs a well-planned future, I'm not implying you have to know what goes in volume 67, number 4, in the year 2065. But you need to know if your concept will be relevant in five or ten years.

HAVE FUN!

In the end, remember to have some fun. If you're not enjoying yourself, neither are your readers.

You heard it here.

Rand Ragusa is founder and publisher of Tribe *magazine, based in New Orleans, Louisiana.* Tribe, *the Generation X guide to life, music, fashion, and entertainment for the city of New Orleans, had its first issue in October 1995.*

Interview:

Rand Ragusa
Tribe

You came up with the concept for your New Orleans-based magazine while living in Amsterdam. How did you do this? What were your primary challenges?

TimeOut Amsterdam was sort of a hip, cutting-edge publication that told me what was going on in and around the city of Amsterdam. I had always been a big magazine reader anyway, but I really fell in love with this publication. I lived there for five years, and I became really attached to this magazine and waited for it every month. I wanted to find out what was going on, whether it was bars or bands or restaurants.

I came to New Orleans in the summer of 1994 on a vacation and there was no *TimeOut New Orleans*, and there was nothing that resembled *TimeOut Amsterdam*. There was, of course, *New Orleans Magazine*, which is your typical city publication with your typical museum and restaurant listings, something my grandmother would be interested in picking up if she were visiting New Orleans. But there was nothing that spoke to me.

I finished my vacation here, went back to Europe, and somewhere along the way I began to think, "God, maybe I am ready to move back to the States." I had been in the financial industry for seven years. Ever since I finished school, I had been a trader in global commodities. I thought, "God, am I going to do this all my life or do I want to do something more challenging in something that I have no concept of? Should I embrace something that was almost a complete 180-degree turnaround? Should I give up my educational background for something new?" And that's when I thought maybe I would like to start publishing a magazine.

I knew nothing about publishing, and there was no guide on how to start a magazine. I did probably four or five months' worth of research in the magazine industry—success rates, ad pages versus editorial pages—and really began to learn bits and pieces about why I should not start a magazine. Basically, everywhere you go, people let you know up front that the percentage of magazines that survive, even within the first two or three months, is probably 5% to 10%. The amount that start and survive in the first year is even smaller than that.

So telling my parents that I was going to move to a city that I knew nothing about and had never lived in, yet I was going to do a magazine there about that city, was very confusing to them. "How dare you think you can do this, you know nothing about publishing, you know nothing about advertising, you know nothing about journalism, you know nothing about printing, you know nothing about paper, you know nothing about New Orleans, what makes you think you can do this?" Truly, it presented the ultimate challenge to prove that everybody was wrong and that I could do this if I put my mind to it.

Fortunately, I had earned a good living while I was in Europe, and I had the money saved away because I knew that it was going to take a long time to figure out the city, first of all. I had to figure out who I could trust, figure out who was the true talent, because I knew that I was going to bring a business background to the table. The magazine world is a merging of the artistic world and commerce.

You must have some sort of business sense. You should approach it with the philosophy that, "I want to start a magazine because advertisers would feel that this is a viable outlet for them to showcase their products." Otherwise, don't start the magazine unless you just want to spend money. If it is not an outlet for advertisers to reach a particular demographic, then it's a lost cause.

I felt New Orleans, and the South as a whole, had no magazine that targeted youth culture, meaning 16 to 34 years old. There was no magazine that represented true journalistic integrity that didn't sort of have that old southern tradition to print only those things that don't offend anyone. I felt there was a lot of groundbreaking that was going to have to be done in order for me to do what I wanted to do. I was going to a very conservative, southern city and convince the residents that they needed this magazine from a consumer standpoint.

I was also going to have to convince local advertisers to support such a magazine. They had never been sold on the fact that this young demographic has an economic impact on their business. I was going to have to teach them that this 16 to 34 demographic *does* spend money. Generally, your local advertiser might not be as savvy as a New York agency would be. The Ma and Pa grocery store or restaurant or hair salon doesn't think anybody young has money. They think they don't go out and buy new clothes, that they don't go out and spend money on entertainment. So that presented a major challenge. I had to introduce a new product, and an entirely new concept that wasn't too southern and conservative in nature. And I had to define an entire demographic.

So, needless to say, I was up against a mountain of adversity. Yet I truly felt that the Calvin Kleins and the Levi's and the Coca-Cola's and the Budweisers of the world hadn't been able to reach this demographic throughout the South. I was convinced. Even though Atlanta or Dallas produced a larger market for me, New Orleans had that charisma. It had that captivating presence to it. When you say New Orleans, people's eyes light up. They know New Orleans.

Fortunately, we were able to produce an editorial product that received a lot of national attention. We made companies feel that they had no choice—they had to be in the magazine. But we are still battling. We're on issue 15 and are still carving our niche nationally.

Once, I was on the phone with a sales rep and he kept saying, "Well, aren't you just a New Orleans magazine?" I said, "No, we're sold throughout the world. We are distributed nationwide through Barnes & Noble, and we're pretty much on all the newsstands." But it is hard to overcome that. New Orleans, though it is very magical and people have this fondness for it, it still isn't in the top fifty markets.

To start a magazine like I did it took a lot of planning. I moved here in February 1995 and did not launch the magazine until October 1995. My biggest recommendation to anyone out there is to talk to as many people as you can. I basically would call other magazines and ask for meetings with the publishers and go in there and actually tell them what I was up to and ask if they had any feedback for me. I would let them know that I was not planning on being their competition, per se.

How did they react to this?

I think some people were thrown off. Generally people are quick to dismiss any sort of start-up publication because they know how difficult it is. So a lot of people allowed me to come in, but I am sure that as soon as I left—even though I was convincing and I had desire and I had a plan—I am sure they thought I would never do it. Until we reached our anniversary issue, I don't think anyone thought we could do it. It is probably one of the most difficult businesses in the world to run. You are judged each and every month. You rise or fall on the quality of your product. One wrong move, and people start to lose interest in your product. Then everything that you have done to build up that trust and faith and interest in what you have to say could be wiped out with a single issue. So building a brand name, something that people associate with and want to associate with, is a lot easier said than done.

Tribe is giving people a way of life. It defines a certain look, a fashion. It defines a certain attitude. We do that each and every month. We have to be creative and come up with fresh, clean, intriguing ideas that captivate the audience. It's nearly an impossible task, given the kind of budget that *Tribe* works on. To provide such a quality product, ask writers to write for basically nothing, ask photographers to shoot for basically nothing, ask your staff to work for basically nothing each and every month, and still put out a product that looks like a national publication with a big budget, is very difficult.

It's a complicated task, but being the publisher of a magazine is probably the most glamorous title you can have. And it seems like, especially with a high-profile cosmopolitan title like *Tribe*, people assume I'm going out with all the models and I'm living this high-flying lifestyle. They don't see me vacuuming the office twice a week and taking out the garbage at night and working on weekends and carrying the boxes. You have to be able to commit your whole life to it. It is not a nine-to-five job.

Have you had any regrets along the way?

I can't even think about regrets, because I am so far in financially, and I've asked so many people to commit either their lives or hundreds and thousands of dollars. I have no choice. I am married to the magazine and I have no time for regret or negativity. It is not allowed. There are times when I'm overwhelmed, but, somehow, it seems to be worth it. Every time that new issue rolls around, I know that we are one step closer to being more national than we are already.

There are so many milestones that we've reached and there is so much attention that we have garnered that I never dreamed was possible. I shot for the highest star and we are still reaching.

What is your ultimate goal?

I don't know. I mean, I think we are getting there. In just fifteen issues we already have a pilot for a TV show that MTV is considering buying. I'm building a brand. I'm building a way of life. I'm building a tribe, a universal name that sort of crosses all barriers so that it won't discriminate against race or sexual preference or political orientation. It's sort of the wave of the future.

And I think the word *tribe* describes and defines it in a single word. I think we can build a TV program. We can build a publishing empire, if you will. We started out throwing a party for twenty people, and now we throw parties for two thousand people. If you don't get an invitation to a *Tribe* party you just are not in.

Tell me about these parties.

These parties that we throw are our way of giving back to the community in exchange for creating an image. Everything we do is about image. You cannot just roll into a city like New Orleans, especially one that has an old guard. They won't allow you in. And if you make any mistakes or burn any bridges, people don't forget. When we came to town we had to be very careful, very courteous to any and all people that we dealt with. We never bashed competition.

We realized that we had a very delicate situation. Nobody wanted to sell our magazine because we were too controversial. So you can imagine the amount of doors that were closed, but we felt that if we came in and we were honest and worked hard, people would have to accept us.

Did they?

Without a doubt. You make mistakes along the way, but the trick is that you learn from them and never ever forget them. One party that we threw had an advertiser called Cybermind, and it was sort of the virtual reality theme park that had about ten of these virtual reality machines that you put these head gears on. They wanted to trade out an advertisement for a party and it was around Christmas time and we thought, "Oh, wow, wouldn't this be a very year-two-thousand-ish type thing to do? Let's have our Christmas party at this place." Wrong. First of all, you don't throw a party during Christmas for a new magazine—nobody will come. They have too many other powerhouse parties going on with well-established companies or bars or whatever you have to compete with. One of the tricks to me about throwing parties is knowing your competition. Reevaluating, picking a new venue, starting at a place where we can actually control the environment and create the mood. And boom, we landed. We had perfect artwork for the invitations. It was the official premiere party and we were set. Word got out that if you missed that party you missed a very cool party.

The next party was held again at Christmas, but this time we had been in business for a year—thirteen issues—as opposed to two issues, and it was another big success. Actually, Super Bowl weekend, we threw a party for two thousand people for the world premiere of Tribe TV. Now it is set in stone. We have come full circle and that helps. It all creates an image of guys who have worked hard, and people respect that. They know that we came in under adverse conditions and we didn't give up and those that were naysayers, we pretty much shut them up at this point. And that is important too because you have to get support from your local community. Whether you are publishing a magazine about a city or a statewide or regional magazine or an industry specific magazine like *Football Magazine* or *Boxing Magazine*, you have to have the support of the local community around you. You can't rely on graphic designers and writers and people from out of state to produce a magazine, so I think it presents such a challenge to recruit the right kind of people to join.

It took me seven months to recruit my staff. You have to go out and convince them that here is this ten-page document that gives you an overview of what I want to do. Take this home, read it, and meet me for coffee in three or four days. For them to take you seriously first of all— "Why do I want to waste my time? I am one of the top graphic designers in the city—why do I need to come and work for you? I don't need to come and work for you, I don't need to come and write for you, I don't need to come and sell advertising for you. Who are you? You are not even from here. Do you have any money to do what you say you are going to do?" That is where you are, at the beginning; you are at the point where you have to convince yourself that you can do it, you've to get a game plan together because you have to use that to recruit your talent and you have to use that same document, minus the financial numbers, to go out and recruit the talent. So you have a document for recruiting talent and one for industry. They both have to paint the picture. The document in the early stages of the idea is the most critical. I basically committed more than a year to developing the idea.

Is there anything you would have done differently?

I don't know. Probably. I launched an ambitious 10x12

size, which is oversized and very expensive to produce. I wanted to get people's attention. I wanted to be different. I wanted to reach out and grab them. I wanted it to sit on the newsstand and make a statement. I didn't want to be lost in the sea of magazines. So I don't know if I regret that. I think by the third issue we switched sizes. Did that hurt us by switching sizes? I don't think so. At the time I was very apprehensive about doing it but I knew that I could not afford to print a 10x12 magazine any longer. I had to use my economic senses. You have to weigh out the pros and cons, you have to let logic win over any decision. Sometimes you will make an ambitious move with so many risks. There is no way to go back and second guess things.

Has being in the magazine business disciplined you?

I think you have to come into it disciplined. If you are not disciplined, then don't get into the magazine business. I certainly didn't learn discipline by being in the magazine business. Have I learned patience? Have I learned that dealing with the artistic mind presents a whole new set of challenges versus the economic mind? When you are in the business world, you are dealing with a certain mentality and you become accustomed to that mentality. In the artistic world, you are dealing with passion. You are dealing with people who have spent two months writing that article and when you tell them that article is not good enough or that it needs to be changed, it is hard to understand first of all how much effort went into that and why people get upset if you didn't use the photographs they thought you should have used. So dealing with the artistic temperament presents a challenge. And you have to be trusting of other people around you. The talent that you recruit is so important because you can't do it all yourself. So you have to delegate authority, you have to allow people to earn their positions, and once they have earned them you have to turn things over and let things go and give them a chance to work. I ran into a situation with *Tribe* where I had to turn over all of the editorial direction, and I had an editor for six or seven months who put the magazine in a direction that I was not happy with. The magazine improved from all aspects, from ad sales to the design of the magazine, but the editorial content just didn't climb the ladder like the other things did. It didn't improve at all, and so nine issues later I had to fire the editor. Right now I have a new editor. I have defined the parameters and he understands that I have the final say, but he knows that I trust him enough that if feels that it should go in the magazine then I am going to allow him to do that. If I don't trust him, he is never going to develop that confidence he needs to do his job. It is a very delicate situation, and I recommend that anybody starting a magazine recruit talent. You are never going to get everybody right. You are going to have to be able to fire people, even people who have been with you a whole year and have worked for you for nothing.

Given the grueling pace of magazine publishing, how have you avoided burnout?

I am worn out right now. In fact, after twenty-seven months of working on this project, I am taking my first week of vacation next week and I can't tell you how badly I deserve it. I sort of feel guilty that I am taking it.

Why is that?

I don't know. I trust everyone here and I am reachable by pager and I am going to bring my computer.

That is not a vacation.

Well, I cannot just totally detach myself. I have to be there to make the decisions. There are some things that just don't happen until I give the final nod and that is just the way it has to be. Because I am the one who knows best. I am the one who has been here the longest and I know where we are going. At least I have to *act* like I know. You have to expect other people to commit the same kind of time and effort that you do, but probably you hire five or six people as designers, editors, secretaries, bookkeepers, and you hope that at least 50% of them will still be with you after the first year. If they are, I think you have done a good job picking that initial crew.

One of the things about magazines is that the longer you are in business, the better chance you have of recruiting better talent. After you have been in business a year and have shown some stability and you have shown the design community and your city that you are producing this quality product, then you are going to have topnotch designers interested in coming on board. You have to be open to change within your staff, and you have to be aware that the magazine is an evolving product. It is going to take different directions when you bring different people in, and you must allow it to change. I have defined the roles of my staff, and I have defined what I expect them to do and what I expect to see each and every month. At the same time, yes, I am open to new ideas and please bring them to me.

Today is a prime example: I walked into my editorial staff and said I want you to think about this, each and every one of you. What about losing the New Orleans tagline on the cover of *Tribe*? So now, it is not just *Tribe* magazine from New Orleans, it's *Tribe* magazine, and that is it. Now everybody will know, especially the people who followed the magazine from the beginning, that it is from New Orleans and our editorial content will embrace New Orleans and the southern way of life. But do we really have to say New Orleans on the cover?

Is the perception that *Tribe* is a New Orleans only magazine? Maybe so, and is that something that we really want? What do we have to sell here? We are taking the New Orleans way of life and we are selling it to the world. We may sell more magazines on the newsstand because we have New Orleans plastered on our cover. There are some pros in that, but I wanted the staff to think about it, to get their input, to see what their argument would be, to keep it or not to keep it. Because maybe their thinking is better than mine.

The best test for determining whether this concept of yours is a magazine or a book is by developing the contents.

THE CONTENTS

4

Avoid putting the cart before the horse. Sometimes, yes, it can be fun researching the audience and the potential advertisers and the potential competition, but stop wasting your time. Find out if your launch is what you promised it would be before you throw away any more resources. Develop your contents.

Generally, a magazine is divided into three major sections: departments, features, and columns. Anything you can think of will fit into one of these categories.

DEPARTMENTS

The departments in a magazine are the items that will repeat themselves issue after issue using the same title, such as the letters to the editor. You can rest assured that every issue will contain this department in which readers mail comments to the magazine concerning the prior issue or issues. The content changes, but the department stays the same.

FEATURES

The features are the articles that will change from issue to issue. In your magazine *Ballpoint Pen Illustrated*, you may include a lengthy piece on Bic one month, and the next month you may focus on "Why Pens Can't Write Upside Down." Different pieces, but both are features.

COLUMNS

The columns are the voices of the experts. You will reserve this space for famous or otherwise respected individuals to lend their voices to your publication. They validate the magazine and give it an air of authority. You wouldn't let some weekend warrior with a set of golf clubs write a column about playing the links. No! You'd try to swing Tiger Woods or Jack Nicklaus into doing it.

Departments are the skeleton that holds the publication together.

Departmental Voice

Every new magazine will rely on its departments to establish the tone and voice of the publication. They are the only things that will appear on a regular basis. People will look for them, and they will be there. Readers put faith in them. Departments are the skeleton that holds the publication together. You may change your weight, you may change your percentage of fat, you may change your hairstyle, but your bones will remain the same.

A Baker's Dozen

On average, in a new magazine there are twelve to thirteen departments, each one running only a page or so in length. There's the letter from the editor (only a page), the table of contents (one or two pages), etc.

Counter Intelligence

The best way to determine what departments will be best for your publication is to run out and see what the other guy is doing. Spy. Snoop (but stay legal). Do whatever you have to do to take what they include and make it better. There is no shame in that.

Nirvana

As magazine readers (if you don't count yourself in that

lot, start now), we sometimes fall into the trap of becoming too cozy with our favorite departments, thus forgetting there will be something different every time. If you reach this pathetic stage, as I have many times, you become a member of their cult. You don't care what it says, just as long as you've got your hands on it. Ah, reader nirvana. You're exactly where the magazine staff wants you. If *your* magazine can achieve this level of reader devotion, you've got it made in the shade.

Acid-tested Features

The second key to your publication will be the features. These articles most clearly exhibit your concept. Remember what we said about the lighthouse and veering off course? Here's the proving ground. Run each article through the acid test. Does it sing along with the mission statement of your magazine, or does it require a stretch of logic and a shoehorn to fit in?

Run each article through the acid test. Does it sing along with the mission statement of your magazine, or does it require a stretch of logic and a shoehorn to fit in?

Avoid *Crime and Punishment*

In most new magazines, you will find seven or eight features per issue, each running from four to six pages. Please, please, please don't include articles of more than six pages. It's hard enough capturing the reader's attention for six. Anything more than that and it may as well be Dostoevsky.

Expert Columnists

The third key to your new magazine's content will be the columns. As I said earlier, shoot for the experts. Don't ask Julia Child to write about drag racing. Quiz her about quiche.

The Voice of Authority

Your columnists must be the authority figures on the subjects at hand. Remember, there is a difference between writing an opinion and writing a column for a magazine. George Will is qualified to write a column for the last page of *Newsweek*. If he zings off an angry tirade to the *New York Times* about the Manhattan mass transit system, he's writing his opinion. The fact that you are identifying the author over the content is essentially you, the editor, saying, "This guy knows what he's doing!"

Please Mooch

Immediately determine the experts in the field. Will people care what these folks have to say? It would be like paying Murray Lender to write a column for *Bagels Today*. The man knows his bread, and people know him. It is crucial, then, to ride his coattails early in the process. Build on his credibility and authority. Your young, unproven magazine will benefit from the residuals.

If you read about a cure for cancer in the *National Enquirer* and in the *New England Journal of Medicine*, which one are you going to believe? What if it's the same article, the same exact words? This is why it is so crucial, until your magazine reaches maturity and develops credibility, to have other voices of authority attached to it.

ASK FOR A DIVORCE

The first real step toward determining whether you have a book or a magazine is to divorce yourself from the contents. If you stay away from the writing of the contents, you are admitting you do not know everything about your topic. Even if you do know everything, you cannot write every department, every column, and every feature. If you *can* do this, you've got a book.

Variety Is the Spice

This should be the brightest red-flashing danger signal of them all. Though you may be able to do it all, it is the variety of content, style, and approach that gives a magazine its flavor. As editor and publisher, you have to be the heartbeat. As idea generator, you are the heartbeat. But you cannot manufacture every organ of the body. You must create ideas that others can execute.

PLAN AHEAD

The second step toward establishing your magazine is to

think about the future. When developing a table of contents, usually you must plan at least six months ahead of time. If you're publishing a food magazine, and you have this brilliant way to position a strawberry pie in a strawberry patch on the cover of the July issue, you need to get in gear in December to get the story assignment out. However, there are no July strawberry patches in December. Therefore, you must use a photo of last July's strawberry patch. A whole year in advance! Magazines like *Better Homes and Gardens*, *Good Housekeeping*, and *Southern Living* are planned this way.

As an editor, you must be thinking constantly of the future. Don't plan for the present.

As an editor, you must be thinking constantly of the future. Don't plan for the present. You may be asking, "How can I predict the future?" Don't predict it—live in it and envision what you would like to be reading. For help, look at the last several July issues of your competitors and see what they included besides strawberry patches.

FIND GOOD FREELANCERS

The third crucial step in developing your content is digging up names of freelancers. Who is going to deliver your content? And remember, there's more than articles in magazines. There's photography, illustrations, graphic design, etc. Who will take your photos? Who will draw your illustrations?

Plunder

Again, look to the competition. With *Longbows & Recurves*, I had the publisher look at all the other hunting and outdoor magazines on the market and make a list of all of their writers.

Construct a Database

Check out the staff writers for the competition, which means they cannot write for you, and see who the freelancers are, which means they would be dying to write for you because that's how they put food on the table. You need to put together a database of the people who specialize in your area of interest. Do the same thing for photographers and illustrators. Find out who's doing what.

Trust me, 90% of your magazine will be generated by free-lancers. No publisher in the proper frame of mind will hire a complete staff to launch a new magazine. There is plenty of good freelance talent available. The commitment of hiring somebody for a first issue is too great. If you go belly-up early on, what will you tell your publisher's assistant, his wife, and their several hungry children? "Gee, we can't continue this, so bye-bye."

USE THE DATABASE

The fourth step in developing content is to take your database and put it to use. Contact each and every person on your list. Talk to the writers and use them as a sounding board. See what they think about your idea. Ask for opinion and feedback and review with them some of your proposed content. You need to gather as many ideas as possible.

Remember, these people need you. You'll be surprised at how many ideas are generated this way because you're knee-deep in their area of interest. They've been working on it for years, thinking of articles they'd like to write but never had the chance. You are their meal ticket. You, in return, need to defend your concept, to compare their ideas to your mission. Remember the lighthouse!

These freelancers will help you develop a database of story ideas. This will be crucial as you move into the next phase: specific content generation for your business plan.

HOW MANY IDEAS?

How many ideas do you need to come up with? There is no limit. The more ideas, the better your magazine will be. If you have a thousand ideas, but you need only ten, imagine how focused your publication will be.

Hash It Out

First thing, sit down and hash out every one of your departments. Write a brief description of each department's mission and compare it to the concept.

A Year's Worth

Second, jot down every article that will appear in the first year's worth of issues. Consult your idea database, look to the competition, discuss it among friends ... whatever you have to do. Write the title of the article and what it will be about, who will write it, and what kind of art will accompany it.

List Columns

Third, list your columns and columnists. Write a brief description of who these experts are and what they will be writing about.

THE REST IS EASY

Remember, the people reading your business plan are money people, investors. They may know nothing about hunting raccoons. All they may know is that you are an investment, and they want to know when they will get their money back.

So, once you've followed the steps in this chapter, the rest is easy. You already know exactly what will be in the first issue, the second issue, the third issue, and so on.

All you need now is money.

NOTES

· ·

· ·

· ·

· ·

· ·

· ·

· ·

· ·

· ·

· ·

· ·

· ·

· ·

· ·

· ·

· ·

· ·

· ·

John Floyd is editor-in-chief of Southern Living, *the quintessential guide to life in the South, published by Southern Progress Corporation, in Birmingham, Alabama. In the last two years, he oversaw the launch of the new regional* Living *magazines within* Southern Living.

Interview:

John Floyd
Southern Living

You were not around for the actual launch of *Southern Living* in February 1966, but you were for the launch of *Carolina Living.*

Yes, you're referring to the *Living* magazines, which are actually magazines for individual states within the pages of *Southern Living*.

How did these come about?

Well, it was not my original idea. I really give Don Logan, who is now the chairman of *Time* and former president of Southern Progress, the credit. He always thought that if we could bond more closely to our readers and the things they like, we would be better off.

He always had the idea, "What if we did a magazine just for North Carolina or just for Tennessee or just for Georgia or just for Texas, which talked about the people and places?" *Southern Living* tries to help people understand how a home is decorated, the architecture of the home, and talks about it from the perspective of the people living in that state. It makes these things a source of pride.

Then he thought that we had a tremendous tool not only to grow the circulation in that state, but also to attract a different type of advertising—mainly the retail portfolio of advertising that national magazines probably would never attract because they were only going after national business.

That was his idea, and I'll have to say, it took us a long time to come around to saying, "OK, let's try this idea." We tried it first in North Carolina.

Why did it take so long?

You have things that you tend to want to do. I became editor a number of years ago, and Don went off to *Time*. It is just a matter of the evolution of a product in a magazine and having the right people in place and figuring out the system to do it.

When you are dealing with a big magazine, candidly, the wheel can turn very fast on certain things or turn very slowly. It takes a newly structured organization to handle *North Carolina Living*, and we did not have all that in place. The plan was for us to get our ducks in a row, advertising and circulation had to get their ducks in a row, and all had to come together and say, "Yes, we can do it," and all work hard to make it happen.

What bumps did you encounter along the way?

One of the problems we encountered was a sales staff that was not geared to sell, was not ready to take advertising in the sense of calling on retail advertising. So we had to develop a new way of doing that.

Editorially, we had home, garden, travel, and food people who covered states, but we did not have people to cover features within a specific state. So we had to develop a new system. We actually formed a new department called our Features Department. We decided we would assign an editor a *Living* section, and under that we have been 99.9% staff produced.

We had to figure out if we should continue being staff produced, or should we do some collective freelance.

We decided to do some collective freelance with some people we knew and trusted.

And then came photography. We realized we had to have a new generation of photography for these magazines. So we had to designate a whole series of *Living* photographers. We were fortunate to have people on staff to fill the positions.

Then came all the manufacturing and problems like how you are going to put it in the book and make it work. We had all the typical pains of a new editorial product, just as you would a new magazine. The only thing the *Living* sections have that a new stand-alone would not is built-in circulation. There were no media circulation headaches. Besides that, there was nothing unusual in the development and launch.

How do you think the *Southern Living* **circulation base helped the** *Living* **launches?**

Well, we had a very good circulation in North Carolina. What we did know was if this worked we would be very comfortable expanding our circulation in North Carolina. I will tell you, the reaction of the readers was very well-received, very appreciated. We saw very positive results from our renewal effort there. The reader reaction was, "Hey, this is something that nobody else has done and they really care about us."

I think the reader reaction effectively increased the overall volume. It actually became a plus all the way around in the circulation of readers. I think they would agree.

I think North Carolina was selected to be the first one, too, because we have such strong roots there and such a strong component of loyal readers there. So we wanted to build on our strength.

Did you do any test marketing beforehand?

No, not really. We certainly talked to a group of people, a group of our internal staff, and we took some editorial surveys just to see if there was some room for these kinds of subjects in their minds, and there definitely was.

But as far as formal focus-group testing, we really did not do that because, quite honestly, the more we looked at it, the more positive it became. We really did not see a downside. Luckily, everything about it was an upside. The June 1997 issue had sixty pages in the *Carolina Living* section—a very handsome edition to the two-hundred-page book.

What about advertisers? Was there any reluctance on the part of the advertisers?

Not really because we have such a terrific name. We have high name recognition. It became a pathway for advertisers that we have not had in the past. It is very, very good.

Our biggest problem with the advertisers is our ability to call on the people we need to call and then service them. We work hard at doing that.

We had very positive results, even on the first issue. We had agreed on an editorial base number regardless of advertising, and, quite honestly, we did almost 50% advertising in the first issue.

If you set that as a goal for a base, and you get the ad ratio at 50/50, you are pretty doggone successful right out of the shoot, instead of going down with the second issue. I think the second and third are really key issues. We constantly added editorial pages to the third issue. That was a pretty good sign in my mind.

What advice would you give someone who is trying to recruit advertising?

Know your marketplace, and know your goals. We believe that focus is everything. Focus on your product from an editorial perspective, focus on your market from an advertising perspective, and be able to have confidence to tie the two together in making a successful, strong presentation.

I believe that is the most outstanding characteristic we had. We were all together on what we wanted to do and how this could help our readers and, in turn, help our advertisers. It became and continues to be a reader-based product, not an advertising-based product.

It is so easy today to become an advertising-based product versus a reader-based product because of the pressure. If you don't have the readers, you really are not going to get the advertising.

So you launched *Carolina Living* and that went well. What came next?

Tennessee, and it did equally well. Tennessee is a very different kind of state than North Carolina. It looks very similar, but if you start dissecting it from a business perspective, it is a little bit different.

We used the same pattern, the same format, the same folio, and got a lot of play. We did have a little more competition in Tennessee than in North Carolina, though. Matter of fact, we had to apply for the rights to the name *Tennessee Living*. But, basically, it worked the same way as *Carolina Living*.

Then we started *Georgia Living*, which was very different. With North Carolina and Tennessee, you have a diversity of cities—Charlotte and Raleigh, and Knoxville, Chattanooga, and Nashville. In Georgia, you have Atlanta, and then everything else, in sort of a funny kind of way.

So when we got to Georgia, we had a very different set of perspectives. You have this mass of cities and then you have all the great cities of Georgia, but you also have this overriding 50% of all the population of Georgia, which lives within an hour of the Hartsfield airport.

So you have a very, very different situation in which you have to position your product. Georgia became a very intriguing experience. We had to decide how we would cover the state. If you look at the product, we are doing that well. We are certainly making sure Atlanta gets all of its due, but Atlanta is not going to be the whole magazine. The whole state is included.

Georgia Living exceeded its estimated editorial pages on the first issue and has never been below that mark. That is the way it is running.

So as we move to Texas, I think you can readily see that we are excited because it is our biggest circulation state. We think we are going to bring incredible dimension to Texas.

How can *Southern Living* grow even more?

The growth of a magazine needs to come in a lot of arenas—renewal rates, circulation, newsstand sales. Right now, we are at 2.4 million. We would like to go to 3 or 4 million eventually.

In the advertising arena, I think it goes unsaid. I see a tremendous dimension, and I expect that to continue to grow. In editorial, there are just numerous ways I would like to grow. Not only in the addition of more *Living* sections, but we would also like to be more creative in growing some of our culture, garden, and travel sections.

We would like more regional growth and specialization. To me we are in our infancy of growth, not at our high point in growth. I think our approach of staying in the middle class, on the positive side of things, is a dimension not being duplicated by other magazines.

What about the new, digest-size publications?

We have one, called *Southern Living Recipes*, which is a digest recipe book. We are very excited to put this on the market. We went into a year of testing in 1996, and by 1997 we continued growth on the newsstand and the newsstand only. We are learning a great deal.

We think it is an outstanding format for recipes, and we actually offer more recipes than any of the competing magazines. We are publishing ten this year, and we think the marketing potential in the long term is very, very favorable.

We think people subscribing to *Southern Living* and then buying this on the newsstand is a very logical progression. Especially with a single topic of interest, such as Mexican food.

The biggest thing for us to remember is to maintain that quality quotient at the level of the main book, *Southern Living*. From our perspective, we feel very good about that. We know that the market is, for us, a new venture. But we also think it is the kind of future which, especially at *Southern Living*, our editorial side can be very creative with.

We have really learned a lot going from an 8½x11 to the digest. It takes a whole new generation of thought process, too. You don't just shrink the books. You literally have to formulate how a recipe is going to look in there. And you have to maintain every quotient, like graphic design.

We feel very good about it in its second year. I hope, if you call me in five years, I would say we are in year seven. That is what our goals are. We committed a great deal of staff time and dollars to making this successful.

NOTES

....

....

....

....

....

....

....

....

....

....

....

....

....

....

....

....

....

This is as good a time as any to teach you some manners. Not to say you're rude, but when introducing your magazine to the general public, there are a few particular p's and q's you need to mind.

INTRODUCING YOUR MAGAZINE

5

As I run through this "to do" list, remember that magazines have changed. As you saw in the **Market Overview** chapter, magazines can no longer be all things to all people. Instead, they have become niched and microniched. In the truest sense of the phrase, magazines speak to the "audience of one" now more than ever.

LETTERS FROM THE EDITOR

As a result, editors and publishers are falling all over themselves to be as personal and friendly as possible as they hone in on the demographics and psychographics of their readership. The letter from the editor in your premiere issue is where it all begins.

Over the years, I have noticed twelve elements common among first-issue letters from the editor:

• **Include an introductory sentence and thank-you note.** "Hi there," wrote Kit Keifer, editor of *Investor's Guide*. "I thought that would be a better way of starting this magazine."

• **Describe your preparation work.** Here, editors often indulge in their war stories of how the magazine was conceived in less than six months, or three months, or even in one month. "I thought we could devote a few months to research and then produce a premiere issue of *WinTech* in July 1992," wrote J.D. Hildebrand, editor of *Windows Tech Journal*. "We decided to accelerate our plans—to produce this premiere issue in a scant three months. We worked around the clock for six days.... We squeezed a year of work into the next couple of months."

Editors like to believe that their magazines are more than just ink and paper. They reflect reality. They teach people how to live.

• **Link the magazine to reality.** Editors like to believe that their magazines are more than just ink and paper. They reflect reality. They teach people how to live. Thus, it comes as no surprise that editors, in their opening letters, try to emphasize the fact that their magazines reflect exactly what is going on in society. "This past year," wrote Joseph A. Gallo, executive editor of *Card Collector's Price Guide*, "one could hardly but notice the increase in non-sport card activity... at shows, in advertisements, and especially in new set productions."

• **Outline the magazine's concept.** Here, the editors state what they plan to offer in their magazines. They lay out their righteous missions for the reader. "When I first conceived of this magazine," wrote Casey Exton, editor-in-chief of *Tattooing by Women*, "I decided that it would be the fairest, most democratic presentation of female tattoo artists possible. I wanted *Tattooing by Women* to be just that—women's work."

• **Explain the essence of you.** This is where the editor takes a little time out to stroke the reader's ego—always a worthwhile pastime. "The first issue of *ShopNotes* was born of a trait common to all woodworkers," wrote Donald B. Peschke in the first issue of *ShopNotes*. "We like to talk about our shops, the tools we use, the techniques and the way things work. If you like working in your shop ... this magazine ought to appeal to you."

• **Identify the reader.** This can be very delicate. You want to be as specific as possible, but you don't want to alienate any secondary readers. Therefore, most editors refer to their readers in general terms. "Having already assumed that you are, as I am, a recruiting enthusiast (why else would you be reading this magazine?)," wrote Jeff Whitaker, editor of *Deep South Football Recruiting Guide*, "I'm also going to assume that we're interested in the same kind of information in a recruiting publication."

• **Stand out from the crowd.** With the thousands of titles already on the newsstand, editors have caught on that differentiation is the key to success. They have to establish that, not only are they different from the rest, but they're also better. "What makes this wrestling publication totally different from every other magazine on the newsstand today is one very, very important fact," wrote Michael O'Hara of *New Wave Wrestling*. "I am a wrestling fan, and this magnificent masterpiece is put together by wrestling fans for wrestling fans."

• **Make promises to the reader.** The editor must make some campaign promises to the reader. He must lay out in full view his intentions for the future of the magazine. "*Earth* will show the planet and give you the intellectual tools for getting to know it better than anyone has before you in the history of time," wrote Steve Zaburunov, editor of *Earth* magazine.

• **Make requests of the reader.** There are always questionnaires that need to be filled out and returned or advice that needs to be solicited, but there is also a group of more casual requests you can make that will benefit the magazine. "Remember," wrote Gareb S. Shamus, publisher of *Wizard* magazine, "tell your friends you collect *Wizard*."

• **Boost one's self.** As you've already stroked the reader's ego, it's time to caress your own. This point in the letter is the most common spot for editors and publishers to share some of their real-life stories with the readers. "Like so many of my generation," wrote Randall Jones, CEO of *Worth* magazine, "I had been reasonably good at making money, extraordinarily good at spending it, but not worth a damn at figuring out what to do with it in the long term."

• **Present the contents of the magazine.** By highlighting some of the contents in this premiere issue, you are already making good on that campaign promise made earlier in the letter. "Whatever your fitness level," wrote Janet Figg, editor of *Eating Right, Living Well*, "you'll find information of benefit in 'Spring Training' on pages 19 through 28."

• **Bid farewell.** Like I said, editors are falling all over themselves to make their magazines as personal as possible. To this end, sign the letter as though it were a personal letter to an old friend. Just a few words to express thanks and wish good luck is all it will take. "Best wishes," signed Candy Lee, managing editor of *Harlequin World's Best Romances*.

CONCLUSION

Bear all of these points in mind and the reader will be well-prepared to slip comfortably into your publication. The ultimate goal is to convince this reader, and the one after that, to proclaim, "This is *my* magazine!"

Make your mother proud.

John Sowell is publishing director of the Memphis Crop Division of Vance Publishing Corporation, located in Memphis, Tennessee. He launched Dealer & Applicator, *the magazine of service and management strategies for farmers, in January 1996.*

Interview:

John Sowell
Dealer & Applicator

How did you relaunch *Custom Applicator* as *Dealer & Applicator?*

We first took a hard look at our audience. As *Custom Applicator* evolved, it became very evident that the independent custom applicator was a shrinking audience and the bulk of our audience was made up of fertilizer, crop protection, and seed dealers. As we reevaluated our position in the market, we found our name obviously did not reflect our audience. So we did some research to determine if the name change would have any positive or negative effect, or whether it would have none at all.

How did you do that research?

We used personal interviews, both with advertisers and with over a hundred subscribers to the magazine. And what we found was the name change was not an issue at all. Everyone understood the rationale behind the name change. They were very loyal to the content and insisted that we not change the quality of the content, but a name change would be acceptable.

How did you decide on the name *Dealer & Applicator*?

Our circulation is a little over 16,000, and 14,000 of those are dealers of the various products that I mentioned. Applicators are important as an independent group because there are independent applicators out there and there are applicators who work specifically for dealers. We are reaching managers of the dealership and of the dealer and independent application operation, working directly with a partnership between product sale and application.

Where did you go from there with your relaunch?

It was important, once we did that preliminary research, that we try to ask all the right questions and then determine our true position in the marketplace. We drafted a marketing plan to reposition the magazine. As a part of that plan, we did some additional research where we examined the role of the dealer and the applicator in agriculture today. That clearly affirmed the role of the dealer and the importance of the applicator as a business partner of the farmer.

Once we had that research in hand, we revisited the name change to make sure that our name was following the strategy of our marketing plan. And then we created new promotional pieces and media kits and moved toward redesigning the publication. But the whole process was research, reposition, and redesign. The redesign was a natural occurrence after we refined our position in the marketplace.

Is there anything you would have done differently?

I have a billion things I would have done better the first time. In retrospect, I would have accelerated the redesign process so that we could have tested various design approaches and techniques. While I am comfortable where we are, it would have been nice to receive some additional validation of where we are going design-wise.

From a positioning point of view, we are right on target and have received a great deal of positive reinforcement from both readers and advertisers. I just wish we had a little more time for pretesting.

If someone wanted to start a magazine, what advice would you give?

Do your homework. Know your market. Move with authority and confidence.

Do you think it is harder to launch a trade magazine than it is a consumer magazine?

In a trade publication, you have to carefully evaluate your role in the industry. And to find that role, you must first make sure there is a need.

As a trade publication you are a driver of trends in industries, but consumer publications typically respond to growing trends and needs. I honestly can't say that one is harder than the other, but the point is, you can't fly by the seat of your pants. You absolutely have to know your market phenomenally well and make sure that your position is a needed position and a position that your magazine can drive successfully.

How do you keep in step with your advertisers?

Too many people sell on unsubstantiated strategies that they can't deliver, and the trick is being able to find out what the right strategy is and making sure you can deliver the goods consistently. Remind your advertisers that you're doing that and expose your competition who cannot deliver.

Do you have any tidbits on surviving in the market?

Never get complacent. Play the game aggressively.

And how do you do that?

Never assume that the position you own today is the position you will have tomorrow.

NOTES

....

....

....

....

....

....

....

....

....

....

....

....

....

....

....

....

....

....

Anybody out there? Now it's time to find out who is going to read your magazine. And, more importantly, who is going to be willing to pay for the pleasure.

THE AUDIENCE

6

A magazine is like a three-legged bar stool. Nearly every magazine is supported by three sources of revenue: advertising, subscription sales, and newsstand sales. Of those, you can see there are dual audiences to reach: the readers and the advertisers. In other words, you need to capture the attention of the man on the street so he'll give you money in exchange for your publication, and you need to snare the businessman who will write big checks for the privilege of placing an ad for his company between your covers.

TWO KINDS OF READERS

However, in magazine lingo, the term "audience" refers to the readers. Of these readers, there are two types: the habitual reader and the impulse reader.

The Habitual Reader

The habitual reader gets so accustomed to your magazine that she wants it on a regular basis. She either has a subscription or buys nearly every issue off the newsstand.

The Impulse Reader

The impulse reader, on the other hand, is titillated by

something on the cover of a magazine and buys it on the spot. Usually, he hasn't planned on purchasing the magazine, but the subject matter is so intriguing or sensational that he just has to take it home. How many people have the *National Enquirer* or the *Weekly World News* on their shopping lists? Not too many. But sometimes the covers are so outrageous, they've just got to have it.

One Man's Trash

What is an impulse buy for you may be a habitual buy for somebody else. Once you hit the stage where you've bought, say, *Cosmo*, on impulse a number of times, you may decide the content is consistent enough for you to send in the subscription card. The minute you lick the stamp, you automatically become a habitual reader. Obviously, you cannot have a subscription and still buy it on impulse.

TWO WAYS TO SKIN A CAT

This seems easy enough. You produce the magazine, distribute it to newsstands, people love it, they buy it, and you make a million bucks. But who are these people who can make you rich? Before we can answer that question we have to back up a couple of steps and look at the two different ways people start magazines.

1. Filling a Hole

First, entrepreneurs like yourself smell a need in a specific market and create the magazine to fill that need. John Kennedy Jr. started *George* this way. He felt there were no young, hip political magazines in America, so he started one. Same thing with *Modern Ferret*. Ferret owners are a specific audience if ever there was one, so this magazine burrowed into that specific niche.

2. Digging a Hole

The second way to launch a magazine, as you might imagine, is to create an audience where one previously did not exist. For instance, there is *Southern Living* for southerners, *Yankee* for northerners, *Sunset* for folks on the West Coast, but is there anything for a midwesterner? Would a midwesterner consider himself or herself part of a regional market? Would a magazine about the Midwest fill a need for anybody? Your magazine would identify a specific group of people, it would carve them out of the general population, and would target them as though they had always existed.

So you see, with the first method, you would know that everybody who recently purchased a new computer would probably be interested in your *New Computer Magazine*. But when you launch something like *Midwest Living*, you won't know how many people will identify with living in the Midwest.

SPARE A DIME?

One of the major determinants of success with any new magazine is finding a willing audience capable of paying the cover price. Why do I emphasize the cover price? Because things have changed. Today's new magazines cost about $5.00 each, as opposed to getting 51 issues of *Life* for $7.45 as you could back in the early '70s. One issue of *Life* can now cost you between $2.95 and $3.95, and most new magazines are a dollar or two more than this. If you put out a magazine called *American Pauper* and charge $7.00 for it, you may not sell a single copy.

One of the major determinants of success with any new magazine is finding a willing audience capable of paying the cover price.

DISSECT THE READER

How do we find the audience? First, you absolutely must identify who will read it based on its content. The business plan hinges on this crucial data. You need to compile as much research as you can on your typical reader. The best way to do this is to divide the reader into two parts: demographics and psychographics.

Demographics

Demographics are all the statistical information concerning age, occupation, income, marital status, education—anything you can quantify. If something about your magazine's audience can be reduced to numbers, find it and reduce it to numbers. For instance, your typical reader may be a male between 35 and 55 who is married, has 2.7 kids, makes $750,000 to $1,000,000 per year, and drives a Japanese-made sport utility vehicle.

You can find all the demographic information you need at your local library. Simply ask the person at the reference desk for a copy of the *United States Statistical Abstract* and find yourself a comfortable chair. This 1,000+-page book is put out by the Census Bureau and contains everything you could ever want to know about the United States. It can tell you how much beef we eat, how much gas we use, how many people live under each roof, and how much money people between the ages of 25 and 34 make in a year. The *Abstract* is an indispensable tool for people in the magazine business.

Psychographics

On the other side of the coin, we have psychographics. This is all the information relating to the values and lifestyles of your audience. You may know you want to reach rich people with college degrees over the age of 25, and we may know exactly how many of them are out there, but do we know what they think about abortion, or whether they spend money in big or small chunks, or whether they get along with their families? You need to know these things.

As the magazine's creator, you must be able to convince advertisers that you are hitting readers who will spend money on the goods and services they are trying to sell.

You would much rather have 1,000 big spenders in your audience than 2,000 rich people who don't spend a dime. Remember, the ultimate goals are to get them to shell out for the magazine and to shell out for the items advertised in your magazine. This dual audience system will collapse if you can't convince that second audience, the advertisers, that you are hitting readers who will spend money on the goods they are advertising.

GATHERING DATA

Finding the necessary information may not be the scavenger hunt it appears to be. Try carrying on some informal conversations with folks you believe are in your target audience. Ask them how they like what's available to them, not just on the newsstand, but in all the media. Ask them what they need but are not getting. Who comes closest to providing this?

You will probably know the answers to these questions right from the start, especially if it's a niche market, but it never hurts to check. Incorrect conclusions based on data are easy to make.

For instance, a key question you need to address is, how important is this subject matter to the audience? What is the level of interest in a magazine on this topic? Sure, 200 million Americans probably use paper clips on a regular basis. If you asked every one of these paper clip users what they thought of the subject matter, they'd probably say the paper clip is the handiest thing since belt loops. But would they read *Modern Paper Clip Magazine*? I doubt it. But you may not know this about your specific magazine without speaking to a living, breathing audience member.

Formal Discussions

I recommend moving from the casual conversation stage to the group discussion stage as soon as you feel you're ready for some serious audience feedback. Get about fifty individual interviews under your belt, with everyone from the man on the street to the man in the executive suite adding his two cents' worth. Move from chit-chat over coffee to actual conversation with a legal pad and prepared questions.

Focus Groups

Then bring in the focus group. If you fill a round table with about five or six people—average, everyday people—you'll be surprised at the new insight you'll receive. Alone, someone can unload exactly what he thinks. Thrown together, people will feed off each other, creating a dialogue of points and counterpoints you'll find invaluable. You'll get a better idea of whether they're casual, avid, or rabid followers of your master plan.

A key question you need to address is, how important is this subject matter to the audience? What is the level of interest in a magazine on this topic?

PREDICTING BEHAVIOR

In the end, you'll have gained a deeper understanding of your audience. Think of them as your spouse. The better you know your spouse, the easier it is to predict what he or she is thinking. After a while, you can predict behavior and stay out of trouble. For a magazine publisher and editor, this level of audience comprehension is nirvana.

For a husband or wife, it's an absolute necessity.

Sarah Petite is the editor-in-chief of Out, *a general interest magazine for gays and lesbians published by Out Publishing Inc. The first issue of* Out *appeared in 1992.*

Interview:

Sarah Petite
Out

At what stage and in what capacity did you join *Out*?

I wasn't the founder. The founder was Michael Goff, and the magazine was already established when I came into it. But I worked on the first issue. I helped to launch it. But I started work with the editorial. Everything else was already there.

What type of advice would you give someone who is launching a magazine?

I would probably tell them to walk to their nearest newsstand and take a look to see if what they want to do has already been done. And if it has been done, in what way has it been done, and how are their ideas different?

I think, especially in any major urban area, you can look at any newsstand of any size and find an enormous array of titles on pretty much everything from fly fishing to car mechanics to gay and lesbian lifestyles. For instance, the one I work on had pretty much been covered. But when we launched our magazine, what we noticed by looking at the newsstand was that there were no monthly feature magazines targeted to the gay and lesbian audience, nothing that addressed their issues in a full-quality, industry standard way. So we said, "Well, there's something that needs to be done which hasn't been done and that, obviously, people are going to be interested in."

If you see that there are already five or six people doing it, and you are not going to bring anything particularly new to the story, then you probably won't have too much success. Unless, of course, you are a major magazine company and you can figure out how to squeeze out all of the little guys. But to the entrepreneur, it probably should be something with some necessity behind it.

How can an entrepreneur give the concept that special spin?

I think what we said was, you know there are probably a fair number of gays and lesbians in America. No one knows exactly how to count them, but even a rough estimate certainly puts them at the size of a magazine that is acceptable to launch. Most of the major companies want a magazine to hit about five hundred thousand at the get-go, but it depends on how quickly you are going to increase your circulation. You have got to have a reasonable amount of circulation pretty soon after the launch to be able to warrant your expenses.

I think the way you put the twist on your idea is by finding something unique and special. I think what we found was this group of people who have a lot of common interests, whether that's the more political aspects of what a gay issue is, or whether it's the more cultural aspects of things, or if it's simply the basic questions of how to organize your finances with your partner. Any of those things that are straightforward service questions, as they say in the magazine trade.

We knew that there was no real, centralized place they could go for that information in a consistent way. Doing a magazine such as ours would provide people with a unique publishing product that they probably couldn't get anywhere else. As with any audience, what you want to do is look at your group and say, "What is it about these people that pulls them together? What are their shared interests? And what is it about this product that you are giving them that no one else can?"

You know, obviously for gay men and lesbians, it's even harder because in the past it's been this community of people who are so dispersed. It was harder for them to identify themselves and speak of their common experiences. So, for a magazine, this is a very good thing because you want people who are hungry for information and for what you want to bring them.

Is there anything you would have done differently?

I honestly don't know if I would have done too much differently. I know one thing that is very important is not to grow your magazine more quickly than it can handle. One of the classic ways you can go bust is to grow too fast and too furiously. Don't start laying on a bunch of staff that you can't afford to keep.

When we made our first magazine, we were in the offices of another company. *Esquire* actually offered us the space at Hearst Publications because the man who designed our first issue, Roger Black, had his design studio at *Esquire*. He worked on *Esquire* as their art guru, so we had the space and we had access to computers and it was all for very little money.

We had five or six people who worked on it, but now, five years later, we have a staff of thirty-two, including people from all over the magazine industry. Our publisher just spent eighteen years at the *New York Times* in the business department. Our president was at the *Times* for years, too, and at the *Hartford Courant* before that. We now have people from all over.

You can get competitive and start paying the good salaries later on, but don't get too crazy. I think that is one of the problems that people have. They think that they can launch fancy offices with pretty desks and nice carpeting, but they don't think about the fact that the magazine business is really expensive. Last year, for example, our paper costs went up 60%. That's something that you can't foresee, and if you have too much up front, costs can really kill you.

What advice would you give for recruiting staff?

I think one of the key things is to get people who really feel like they want to come to their jobs in the morning. I think you have to inspire them in whatever way. To our benefit, we were making a magazine that a lot of our staff felt was really important. They personally felt very compassionate about the idea of bringing information to a group of people who had not had that before.

So you have the professional motivation of mixing a good product with a lot of pride. If you can hit people at home and make them feel like they are really doing something important, you can come out with any magazine. You can make a magazine about golf and make people who work with you feel that it's important. Often, I feel that people equate that with young, hungry talent. I don't know if that has to do with age or with point of view, but it's best to not have people who feel like they're doing you a favor just by coming to work.

And there is something to be said for people with magazine backgrounds. I think one of the things that created the biggest problem for the gay press is the thought that, "Oh, anyone can make a magazine." Well, no, not anyone can make a magazine. Part of what makes a good magazine is having people with magazine talent. It's a unique skill, just like any skill.

What's the greatest lesson you've learned from the *Out* launch?

Oh, I wish I had more money! Actually, it's been very interesting. I think that I have learned that money isn't everything, even though I just said it was.

You look at something like the report that when *House and Garden* relaunched this fall from Condé Nast, they spent forty-four million dollars over the course of a year or two. That was just to get to the point of relaunching the magazine, just to get to that one issue. Forty-four million dollars—all for prototypes and staff and shooting stories that they wouldn't use.

There was this enormous kind of front loading of that project, and then I look at what I have. Forty-four million dollars, based on how much money we spent in the first five years, we could be around for the next two thousand years. We're talking about just enormous amounts of money. And then I look at how little I do it with, and I say, "Gee." It really kind of makes you appreciate the value of every dollar. Some of this stuff is just crazy. It doesn't need to be this expensive, but money, unfortunately, is useful and you need a lot of it for magazines, for good writers anyway.

Do you do most of your work in-house?

Most of our writing is freelanced.

Is that something you've done from the beginning?

Yes. We try to work with a pretty broad array of people and keep that mix up. The premise of the magazine has always been that we go to talent from all over the industry— whether people are working for *TV Guide* or *Essence* or *Vanity Fair*—and bring them to *Out* where they can do special stories that are especially relevant. Whether it is the arts writer who can write about books for us or the entertainment journalists who can't do exactly that story where they are based. It's kind of taking people's real world specialties and bringing them to *Out* where they make sense for us.

You know, in some next world, it would be nice to have a broad base of people whom you could pay to keep on retainer. But I think people can be really wasteful with that, too. There are major magazines that can lock up millions of people. They want people to be dedicated just to them, and they pay them huge amounts of money so they don't work for anyone else. That kind of stuff can be ego-driven. And ridiculous, too. Is it really worth it to spend a hundred thousand dollars just to keep someone from writing for anyone else?

What about the actual birth of *Out?* **Who developed the concept and how did it grow?**

The idea was essentially Roger Black's, who was behind the first issues of the magazine. Michael Goff, the actual founder, worked for Roger and they were always working on this idea of what would it be like to start a gay magazine. They had started doing prototypes that were targeting only the male readers, and then they actually decided to expand it and make it for men and women.

After the initial investor was brought on board, that's when I came on and started to open offices about six months later.

During those six months, what types of struggles did you face? Did any of them change your thinking?

I do think that their initial change of audience focus was big because emphasis on demographics is really important. I don't know, I guess the cliché is that launches always lead to big fights, and people change and sort of drop off. We really didn't have a whole lot of that.

I think that once we were committed, that first year we were in business, there really wasn't time for anything else. I think that the good thing about Michael's initial idea, once he had the germ of it, was that the message of the magazine and the focus of the magazine and the content have always been consistent. It's not like it started one way and then it morphed and changed a million times. I think that is the way you lose readers. Michael was pretty clear that we were launching a general interest, national magazine for gay men and lesbians.

I think he knew it was going to be topical; it was going to have features and art coverage and fashion. It was going to be a monthly features magazine that a gay *Vanity Fair* would be. In fact, that was one of our buzz lines. He pretty much kept that vision and we have kept it to this day. I think that is really helpful because people aren't trying to figure out what we are.

I also think it was really helpful that we were considered iconoclastic and weird because it was a gay magazine and the whole structure of how you make a magazine was in pretty classic terms. We were going to make a magazine and we were going to make it for audiences that hadn't had that. So the buzz line that came out of that was a traditional magazine for a nontraditional audience. Now, we weren't trying to reinvent the wheel. We were just trying to drive the wheel to a different place, as it were.

What about advertisers?

I think the main thing is that, in the last five years, we have brought on every major advertising category, from fashion to automotive to electronics. In the past, the gay press had never been supported by any mainstream advertisers, and it was considered to be something that was pretty much impossible.

The buzz word was kind of like, "You will get Absolut and you will get Benetton—and the rest of it, well, you will have to make do with love." And that did not prove to be the case at all. What we showed was that we made a quality magazine, and we had a lot of quality contributors, great articles, great photography. People like Roger Black were behind it, and the people in the industry recognized that, and it kind of trickled down.

I think media buyers and people in the industry had to look at that and recognize, "Here's a great way to reach these people and to target these people in a place we haven't been able to get to until now." Ellen DeGeneres' character coming out on TV aside, there really haven't been that many gay media outlets.

So I think it coincided with a moment in the media when people were looking for a way to find new niche markets, and one of the hot, new niches in the early nineties was the gay and lesbian market. It still continues to be. *Out* majestically came at just about the right time for people. It did it in the same way that ten or twenty years previous, people tried to target the African American industry or the Latino industry.

In that respect, the advertising story became a much richer one than people thought it might because we had everyone from fashion retail to automotive to electronic to expensive liquor and tobacco and a lot of other industry that supports magazines. So, in that way, we were looked at as a test case, and a very successful test case.

How important is flexibility?

You have to have a good message, and you have to be convinced about it. If it's like a square peg going into a round hole, and you are bringing people a message and a magazine that no one wants, and you stick to it, you are just going to go down in flames anyway.

But I do think that if you have a good idea, you've got to stick to it for a while because you won't see much happening overnight. You know, it takes a while for small magazines launching on their own to grow like ours has. We are having our fifth anniversary this year, and I am only just now beginning to feel like our magazine is really taking off. It just takes so long.

When you take carrots and potatoes and chicken and you put it in a pot, it takes a while for the flavor to happen, and it does not happen overnight. If you get panicky, and you bail out before you give it a chance to get going, you are not going to have a very good stew. You just have to keep it going for a while. Obviously, simmering that stew is expensive, and in the magazine world, not a lot of people can sit around and wait for that to happen.

In any battle, the most important strategic element is gathering intelligence on your enemy. The U.S. government knows how crucial its role is in the national defense. It is the same for magazines. If you do not know whom you are up against, you're sure to fail.

COMPETITION

The best place to start your intelligence gathering is on the nation's newsstands. And not just a single newsstand, either. You've got to hit a number of outlets because each one may carry an entirely different selection, and you want to sample the greatest variety possible. Tobacconists carry one assortment, while independent bookstores carry another, and grocery stores still another.

These outlets are so important, in fact, that many companies now consider the newsstand to be the acid test for magazines. In other words, if your magazine cannot make it here, it will not make it at all. Following this line of reasoning, if your competition has a tough time making single-copy sales, perhaps you, too, should rethink your strategy.

The second way to get a handle on your competition is to consult reference books. One of the most comprehensive is the *National Magazine Directory*, published by Oxbridge Communications Inc. This directory lists around 26,000 titles, including both consumer and trade publications. Every category is covered, so if you cannot find it here, it probably does not exist.

Another good source is my annual book, *Samir Husni's Guide to New Consumer Magazines*. And this isn't *just a* cheap plug. Each year, I track every new magazine that hits newsstands from coast to coast, and, along the way, I compile statistics for each category. The book, also published by Oxbridge, is now in its twelfth year of printing, so you may want to look to it to see what the competition has been doing since 1985.

The third solid source for researching your competition is the *Standard Rates and Data Directory*, or *SRDS*. The company's name is Standard Rates and Data Services, and it publishes directories for every form of media in this country that accepts advertising. *SRDS* contains approximately 4,700 consumer titles that have reached what is called the "maturity stage." That is, they have stood the test of time and will be around for a while. The book gives advertisers and ad agencies a good idea of what's available to them. *SRDS* can be a good way for you to research the business side of your competition, because it includes ad rates and circulation numbers.

There are approximately 4,700 consumer magazines that have reached the "maturity stage."

EXPERTS

Among the most underrated sources in launching a magazine are the field's experts. I don't mean magazine consultants. I'm talking about experts in the field you are covering. Chances are, you are not that particular industry's leading expert. Most likely, you've seen a void in a certain market and you wish to fill it, regardless of your experience with the topic at hand.

Let's say you think a magazine on hamster care will rake in the big bucks. You don't know much about hamsters, except that they don't have tails and they're smaller than guinea pigs. You know that's not enough data to start a magazine, so you go to the pet store and ask the clerk if there are any hamster magazines already on the market. If not, you may be directed to an old lady in town who has hundreds of the little critters running around her apartment. Now *that's* an expert. Get her opinion, pick her brain, and watch where you step.

From this kind of person you may be able to get the definitive word that there is no such thing as a hamster magazine on the market. If that's the case, you must find out why. Have thirty publications popped up and failed over the past five years? Or, will you be the genius who revolutionizes the hobby of having hamsters?

TRADE MAGAZINES

Other sources often overlooked are the other trade magazines. *Folio:* is a fantastic source for the magazine industry. Many new editors and publishers forget about *Adweek* and *Advertising Age*, which are geared for advertising professionals. If you've been paying attention, you know this world is one with which you should become extremely familiar. You must know what your advertisers want so that you'll be better able to give it to them. Most of these trade magazines should be available at your local library.

MAJORS AND MINORS

As you stand dumbfounded before a rack of a hundred or more magazines, you may ask yourself which of these publications should worry you. Who here is your competition? To answer this question, we need to break your competition into two parts: the major competition and the minor competition.

Three Questions

To determine who fits where, ask yourself these three questions: Does this magazine have a similar concept, a similar audience, and a similar advertising base? If you answered "yes" to all three, then it is a major competitor. If you answered "yes" to two, then it's minor competition. If you answered "no" to all three, then why are you still looking at it? The point is, you need to run through the newsstands and dissect any publication that might come between you and your readers.

Run through the newsstands and dissect any publication that might come between you and your readers.

Fun with Letters

When I began consulting on *Longbows & Recurves* magazine, the publisher and I charted all the advertising the competition had, all of their editorial content, and all of their freelance writers. Then, for fun, we sent a letter with an attached ad and check to *L&R*'s major competitor. We kindly asked them to run this ad for our soon-to-be-launched magazine. The check was returned with a letter saying they do not accept advertising from competitors. Not only did it confirm that they were a major competitor, but it was also fun getting under their skin. We knew we were on the right track.

DETERMINE THEIR CONCEPT

As you study your competition, you must be sure to record their concept accurately. A good place to find it in their own words is in *SRDS*. Each magazine submits its concept to the publication and it is listed just below the magazine's logo. If they are not in *SRDS*, you may be able to squeeze a concept out of the magazine's letter from the editor. The premiere issue is your best bet for such information, but it will occasionally bleed through in later editions as well.

If all else fails, write or call the magazine and ask for a media kit. Tell them you need it for research. If you tell them you are trying to put them out of business, they probably won't send you one. The beauty of the media kit is, not only is it free, but it also contains the concept, the audience analysis, and advertising information.

WRITE A SUMMARY

Once you have gathered all of this information about your major competitors, you can compile a magazine profile for each one. Write, on a single page, everything you know about this enemy. Then, at the bottom of the page, write a paragraph or so about how your magazine will be different. Do this for every magazine you have determined to be a major competitor. For the minor competition, write your profiles consecutively, then sum up the entire lot.

SET YOURSELF APART

It is crucial that you explain how your publication will stand out from this crowd. Remember, you're trying to convince rich people to give you gobs of cash. The more faith you can convince them to have in your concept, the more likely they will be to put money in your bank account. The same thing goes for advertisers. If they can receive the same response from preexisting media, why should they jump ship and advertise with you? Give them something different.

Remember, the creative spirit dominates magazines. More concepts crowd the magazine rack than ever before, so yours needs to be that much more brilliant and better articulated than the rest.

You can do it.

NOTES

. . . .

. . . .

. . . .

. . . .

. . . .

. . . .

. . . .

. . . .

. . . .

. . . .

. . . .

. . . .

. . . .

. . . .

. . . .

. . . .

. . . .

Vaughan Tebbe is publisher of Time Out New York, *published by Time Out New York Partners LP.* Time Out New York *was launched in 1995 and serves as the obsessive guide to impulsive entertainment in the city of New York.*

Interview:

Vaughan Tebbe
Time Out New York

How did *Time Out New York* come about?

Tony Elliott started *Time Out London* about twenty-nine years ago. He came up with that concept just as he was getting out of college. He was frustrated in London at the lack of cohesive information on everything that was going on, so he came up with the idea and started it as a small magazine, basically from his grandmother's kitchen table.

Over the past twenty-nine years, it has grown in London to become one of the largest selling weeklies in the United Kingdom. Tony travels to New York often, and has, over the years, been struck by the lack of a similar publication. There was such an assortment of publications available here, and each one had its niche and had some information, but there was never one place you could go to find all of the things that were going on in New York.

His real passions are clubs and music. He also was always interested in everything else—films, theater—and he remarked that there was no one source for that kind of information.

He had been thinking about this for a long time, and about three years before we launched, some market research was done that supported all of these premises, that there was indeed a void in the market, and that the kind of people who read *Time Out London* would indeed be interested in something like this in New York. So the research supported his thoughts that there was a void.

After the research was done, the business plan was put together, a couple of investors were brought on board, and a limited partnership was established. So it's completely independent. There are no other big publishers involved.

Over a period of maybe less than a year—nine months prior to the launch—the rest of the staff was brought on board from various other publications and locations, but all were currently living in New York. It was staffed completely by New Yorkers, not by anyone from London. But London played a part by consulting with us. You know, just coming over here, interviewing, just to sort of help us get things going.

With the people who were brought on board, we hit the ground running. We hired everyone, from a huge editorial staff of about thirty people, to marketing, circulation, business, production, art, and advertising. And we launched in September 1995. We launched a weekly, which I think is more unusual than usual, because a lot of magazines start with a lower frequency and then build over time. But we just had to be what we were because that was the nature of what we were.

How did you recruit investors and line up financing?

It's a very difficult thing. Our banking firm is the top firm, I think, reputation wise, for the publishing industry, and they put together a business plan. That business plan was shown to a limited group of people.

I think the way that the investors were attracted to the project was that they were very aware of and had used and loved *Time Out London,* and they were personally interested in this project. So a personal interest brought them to it because, for our investors, this is not a huge portion of their portfolio. It's a very small one, so it's almost like their personal part of it.

It's a publication that creates passion in people. They

really come to love it. I don't hear people talk about other
publications the way that they talk about *Time Out London*.
They read other magazines, but they don't just crave it and
say, "Oh, it's the greatest thing. Every time I go to London
I buy it. It's the greatest." And that's what attracted our
investors—its prior reputation.

Did that also help you attract your staff?

Definitely. If we had just launched it as a concept here without ever having any London publications, we would be in
a whole different ball game. It was a huge, huge bonus.

That was one of the things that the research showed. There
was enough of an awareness of the London magazine to
really give us a boost, and that has a lot to do with the
proximity and the closeness of the theater district in New
York and London—the film industry, the music industry,
and how they just sort of feed off of each other and how
New York and London interact. New Yorkers love what
Londoners do and Londoners love what New Yorkers do.
So that really helped feed the whole concept.

What else did you look for when recruiting staff?

Somebody else hired the editorial staff, and she got, literally, more than a thousand resumés without soliciting any.
They all came in when people heard that the magazine
was coming to New York.

Ability was a big factor, not just past experience. In fact, at
a magazine like *Time Out*, experience is not really a factor.
We don't pay what Condé Nast pays. We don't pay what
Hearst pays. We had to look for people who had yet to
really shine. But the person doing the hiring recognized
what she thought were people who were going to shine
and those were the ones she brought on board.

And we basically did that with every department. In
advertising and marketing, we really had to recruit creatively. It's always tough, and you're not at a big magazine. You're an unknown. We really got a lot of young,
energetic, vibrant people who were really excited about
the project, and it reflected very well in the quality of work
that they did, and still do.

What problems did you encounter with advertising?

Everyone wants to wait and see. We didn't have a guaranteed rate base. Normally, when you launch a magazine, you have some sort of subscriber base that you spend a year or two recruiting so when you hit the ground running, you know that you will have "x" amount of sales. Well, we didn't do that.

The original business plan called for launching as a primarily newsstand-based magazine. So we did launch on the newsstands with no direct mail prior to our launch. We had to sell people primarily based on a concept.

We were coming into a very crowded and a very competitive market, so people were kind of like, "We don't know, why do we need to advertise here? We already advertise in the *Village Voice*, we already use the *New Yorker*, so we already have a New York magazine. We don't really need something new."

There were some naysayers, but we still had some supporters. And the supporters were also, in large part, due to *Time Out London*'s reputation. Some of them were common advertisers. In London, some of the biggest categories are film and theater, and that's what developed here as well. But music and theater came on board with us, and some of our initial advertisers who signed on for every single issue signed year-long contracts. This was a huge help.

It was also something that we could take around to other advertisers and say, "Look, these guys signed on for a year." And they were substantial accounts. We really offered something that they didn't have in any other market. There was no other magazine that they could afford to match in advertising. They would have had to advertise in the *New York Times* or the *Village Voice*. This was a new opportunity for them. It was something that we did not have in common with other magazines. They couldn't afford to go to national, big, glossy magazines because there is a lot of wasted circulation. So we offered a unique alternative for a lot of advertisers who wanted a new outlet, or who just didn't have a place to go to get the super enthusiasts for their particular category.

So it wasn't like we were met with welcome, open arms, but we really targeted specific accounts in each market that was important to us. We went after anchor advertisers, and we were able to build it that way.

We also used a marketing approach that was very grass-roots. Again, we didn't have huge budgets. But we wanted to be very much a part of the fabric of New York, very quickly. So we went after local organizations—again, in film, music, and theater primarily, but also in other areas.

We tried to establish marketing partnerships with organizations we felt were very reflective of the spirit of *Time Out New York* and of New York itself. When you want to work with someone on that level, and you approach them with that first, it bodes very well. It's very exciting.

We really wanted to make things work for the magazine *and* the advertisers. Both marketing teams would work hard to make things work, promotional and market-wise, for us and for our partners. Anything we could do for our advertisers that could extend the relationship beyond the pages of the magazine was great. That way, we could tap into their audience or their consumers quickly, which we wanted to do. Being a regional magazine makes it easier to do that.

How did you become involved with the magazine?

They used a head hunter to recruit me and build relationships and get into the market. At the time, I was working at *Details* magazine. Before that, I was working at a company called Miller-Freeman, which is a trade publication publisher. It has many titles in the States and is owned by United Newspapers in London.

I had management experience from Miller-Freeman, and I was just getting into consumer magazines with *Details* when I was recruited. I didn't have the same magazine experience as someone else who was, say, an ad director at some other magazine, but frankly, I don't think it's rocket science. I think that you just have to have some good instincts. You have to be able to follow what you think needs to be done and accomplish things.

I think that they recognized those qualities in me. I was actually hired as the ad director and got promoted to publisher.

What attracted you to the project?

The vast opportunity that it presented. I wasn't, and never have been, a big corporation person who's happy to be a cog in the wheel.

I think that I enjoy sort of having my hands in lots of the parts of the pot. This afforded that opportunity because, in a small operation like this, you wear many hats and you do everything. You have to be really willing to pitch in and wear many hats. Nothing is too mundane for anyone here.

We really have to carry the torch all the time, and that attracted me to it. You are very involved, rather than being distant. It wasn't super departmentalized. Everyone deals with everyone. There is not a huge wall between editorial and advertising. They talk to each other. They're friends.

What problems did you encounter along the way, and how did you deal with them?

I think that there may have been a little bit of a problem with confusion about the product, and, really, communication is what this magazine is all about. There is just so much information, and we have to let the readers know how it all fits into their lives. The people who know it know it's easy, but for the people who don't, it's a little bit more of an education process than we had initially thought. So that is a little more of a problem. It is a problem that we can overcome, but it was more of a problem than I had originally thought it was going to be.

Distribution is always a problem, too. People were always asking, "How are you going to be distributed? The newspaper market is tough. It's impossible to get into."

But as far as the newsstand goes, we got great exposure. Our circulation director was really good at going out and working the stands, and we have great presence.

Economically, we made sense for the newsstands, so we

got great placement. It wasn't like we had to go out and bribe everybody. That wasn't really our problem.

Our problem was more with the post office and getting our subscriptions delivered on time. It was more of a scheduling problem, and that was a big problem. We had to really keep our magazine deadlines very tight because we have a lot of last-minute information that we provide, and we have to print on a very tight schedule and deliver to the post office and the newsstands.

You said one of your problems with advertising was that you didn't start with a set subscription base. Why did you choose to go this route?

It was a combination of the fact that, in London, most every publication is newsstand based, so there was really no subscription experience at this magazine.

At the time, we felt that our strengths were at the newsstand, and that's what we went with. We didn't have a huge budget, and it takes a lot of money to put behind that huge subscription drive before you start. So we chose to use our initial budget to do an outdoor campaign before we launched, so that the people would know that we were there and that they should go to the newsstand to buy us.

I think it was just a judgment call that we could deliver what we needed to on the newsstands and the subscriptions would follow. I think that came mostly from the London experience.

How important was flexibility?

Editorially, we were not really flexible. One thing that I think has been our strength is that we keep very true to our original mission. So there hasn't been any confusion for the readers. We are what we said we were going to be, and we deliver what we said we were going to deliver. From that end, staying true to our mission has been very important to us, and it has been a reason for a successful launch.

I think that some magazines do go through some sort of schizophrenia at first and might not be completely sure, themselves, as to what they are and what they are delivering. I think that they might go through a few different presentations before they establish themselves with their readers. I think that might be a bit confusing, whereas we didn't want to do that. We were very clear on what we needed to be.

As far as everything else, flexibility is very important. You know, we had constant, little daily problems coming at us that we had to deal with as a weekly, and you just have to let them roll off your back. We really had to be creative and flexible to make things work, absolutely.

What advice would you give someone who's launching a new magazine?

That's a really hard one. I think the first thing I would say is be true to your mission. Know your market and embrace it and go whole-hog after it. That doesn't necessarily mean that you have to throw a million dollars behind it.

Work with your market and be a partner to your market so that your market will welcome you. Whether it's editorial, advertising, or circulation, we really went in on every level and established one-on-one relationships.

Not only were our editors having to face, "I want you to do a story."—and the response that they would get would be "Well, who are you?"—they were also having to educate people. Meanwhile, the advertising reps were having to educate people and tell them, "This is who we are." So we really had to establish personal relationships with that market.

We have circulation reps who go around and talk to the vendors every week. We have done that since we launched so that there was a personal relationship and education and awareness that went on at first. The advertising reps were out talking to as many people as possible, trying to get them to understand and be familiar. The editors were out there, too, trying to establish relationships with the right publicists and the right organizations to facilitate the movement of the information.

So I think that is it, really, establishing personal relationships and embracing your market.

What would you have done differently?

I think I probably would have tried to do a little more prelaunch promotion. We basically didn't start our advertising until two weeks before the launch.

How did that hurt you?

I think it probably made everything take longer.

I think that we should have looked at subscriptions a little bit earlier in our life. They are growing great right now, but it's like a missed opportunity.

As I said, we are on the path right now, but if we would have looked at that a little bit earlier, we would have gotten things going sooner.

NOTES

....

....

....

....

....

....

....

....

....

....

....

....

....

....

....

....

....

When it comes to attracting advertisers with your new magazine, there's nothing but bad news. That's why I waited until this far into the book to broach the subject. It's too late for you to turn back now.

ADVERTISING 8

Seriously, advertisers stake their business on advertising response. They want tried and true, not wet behind the ears. What business is going to run up to you and say, "Oooh, you're starting a new magazine? Here's twenty grand. I want in!" This will not happen (unless your monogrammed cufflinks read "JFK").

FREE ADS

So don't get discouraged. It happens to everybody. What you can try is offering an ad free of charge. Unfortunately, there are no statistics on how many premiere issues contain freebies, but I would guess it's a big percentage. You have to say to the national advertisers, "Look how well we fit together." Maybe they'll fall for it and pay for the next one. Or, perhaps, their competitor will pay for one in order to keep up with the Joneses. Bear in mind, some companies won't be interested in a freebie. Would the National Rifle Association want an ad, free or otherwise, in *Utne Reader*? Not likely.

Because you cannot survive on advertising revenue at the beginning, you need to be able to survive based on sales to the reader. So, from the get-go, you need to build your circulation base, not just to pay the light bill, but to attract advertisers in the future.

Of course, there are exceptions. When Condé Nast relaunched *House and Garden*, it sold 275 pages of advertising in the first issue. *George* hit newsstands with 175 total ad pages. OK, those are advertising driven publications. But they are also big names and big companies and have plenty of resources behind them.

I recently worked with a woman from Austin who has been trying to launch *@Austin* magazine. After three months of work, she could only muster three ad pages. Mike Stanley of *Longbows & Recurves* only attracted six pages. The average for premiere issues is eighteen pages, so these are fairly low. But, considering you've got magazines like *George* breaking the curve, some publications wind up with no ad pages at all.

NO ADS AT ALL

This is something we're seeing more and more in the industry. Many new launches are taking the ad-free route because of the hassle and futility of chasing down national advertisers. They just hang it up at the beginning and let the advertisers come when they may. Some survive without advertising for the duration. *Mad* magazine accepts no ads and boasts a circulation of more than a million.

It has only been since about 1990 that circulation revenues have surpassed ad revenues. Even then, they have remained within two percentage points of each other.

THE REVENUE SPLIT

But don't consider this circulation-only philosophy for your new launch. Ads are too good a revenue source to leave by the wayside. For the past five years, established magazines have been ringing up profits at a 50/50 ratio. That is, 50% of revenue comes from advertising and 50% comes from circulation. It has only been since about 1990 that circulation revenues have surpassed ad revenues. Even then, they have remained within two percentage points of each other.

With your new magazine, though, you will likely begin with a 90/10 relationship between circulation and advertising. By year four, you need to bump advertising up to

30% of revenue or else you may be in trouble. This increased ad revenue will be gravy if your circulation numbers steadily increase. Set the 50/50 split as the ultimate goal for your mature magazine.

You need to sit down and draw up a wish list of the big-time advertisers you want to snare eventually.

In the meantime, do not ignore national advertising. You need to sit down and draw up a wish list of the big-time advertisers you want to snare eventually. Imagine two or three years down the road when you can approach anybody you want. You'll have confidence and numbers on your side. Whom do you want on the inside front cover?

CHECK THE NEWSSTANDS

One of the easiest ways to discover who may eventually be in your magazine is to check out your major competition. As you're researching their concept and content, study their advertisers as well. Set your goals based on their ad sales. Seeing which advertisers choose which magazines may help you focus your own concept.

REFERENCE BOOKS

Aside from the newsstand, there are two major sources at your library that can help you research your advertising. They are referred to in the industry as "the red books," but your librarian knows them as the *National Directory of Advertisers* and the *National Directory of Advertising Agencies*.

The *National Directory of Advertisers* lists every single company that advertises anything anywhere. Easy enough. The *National Directory of Advertising Agencies* lists which agencies handle which companies. It also provides a breakdown of where each company advertised, whether outdoor, in newspapers, on television, radio, the Internet, you name it. You need to know where these companies are spending their ad budgets. For instance, alcohol and tobacco companies spend the majority of their money on magazines because of federal restrictions regulating which media can carry their ads. This is good news and you need to know it.

Once you know who advertises where, you need to know that most national advertisers won't give you a second look if your circulation is below about 70,000. Don't be scared. Most new magazines now start out well below this mark. That's why we hit up smaller businesses that don't use ad agencies to handle their work. If you start with a circulation of 15,000, Mom and Pop businesses may be interested. If you start with 500,000, they'd have to fight off Calvin Klein to get space.

MEN FROM THE BOYS

With this in mind, you will divide your ads into two categories: national and Mom and Pop. The national ads, as I mentioned earlier, are for companies that hire ad agencies to create and place all their advertisements. The Chrysler Corporation will accept bids on its multi-million-dollar ad budget, and the winning agency works up a program which, hopefully, will include your magazine. Most account executives at ad agencies have their MBAs now, so you need to be a little more savvy than usual to convince them of your worth. They care more about crunching numbers than they do about the cleverness of your editor's letter.

Mom and Pop companies, on the other hand, do it themselves. You'll probably end up speaking to Mom and Pop in person or on the phone, negotiating a price and handling the money in a couple of easy steps. If you want an ad from Microsoft, odds are slim you'll ever speak to Bill Gates.

For everybody you include in your wish list, you should be able to answer the question, "Why should they advertise?" But don't put it in writing in your business plan. At this point, it's superfluous. Instead, keep it in the back of your mind in case their account executive asks.

All you want enumerated in the wish list are the advertisers you're aiming at and when you will be aiming at them.

Also include what percentage of your magazine's revenue will be advertising at certain points down the road. You may also want to note elsewhere why you want these advertisers. Do they fit your reader profile? Do they advertise in your competition?

THE SALES CALL

When you get around to making the sales calls, life will not be easy. You may have to call five or ten times to convince people to return your message. Even if they do call back, it doesn't mean they will advertise. This is why you must do your homework. If you only get five minutes on the phone with them, you need to make it count. Know your concept backwards and forwards and know your reader's profile like you know your own name. Armed with these two sound bites (and a bus load of passion), you can sell your magazine to anybody.

With magazines, you have to unload your goods on readers *and* advertisers.

Remember, there is no other business in which you have to sell the same product twice. With magazines, you have to unload your goods on readers *and* advertisers. With established magazines, of course, these jobs fall on separate departments. But with your new publication, you'll probably do it all yourself.

REALITY STRIKES

Not only that, but the rejection from advertisers will be that much more personal, as you were likely the one who came up with the magazine's concept in the first place. Just look at it from their perspective. You're asking them to put a great deal of money into something that doesn't even exist yet. The typical answer you'll receive is that they want you to come back in a year.

So do it. Put out a strong year's worth of magazines, then get back on the phone with the same wish list you drew up before your magazine was even born.

You'll be pleased with the results.

NOTES

....

....

....

....

....

....

....

....

....

....

....

....

....

....

....

....

....

....

Marc Smirnoff is founder and editor of the Oxford American, *published in Oxford, Mississippi. The first issue of this general interest magazine of good southern writing hit the newsstands in fall 1992.*

Interview:

Marc Smirnoff
The *Oxford American*

How did you develop the idea for your 1992 launch of the *Oxford American*?

At the time, I was working at a bookstore in Oxford, Mississippi, and, even though we were selling just loads of good southern literature in book form, I noticed there wasn't a good southern literary minded, general interest magazine on the newsstand. By selling all of this and seeing people's interest in southern literature, I thought that a region as big and rich as the South could sustain a good magazine—a magazine that compared to the *New Yorker* or *Harper's*.

Where did you take it from there?

It brewed for a long while, and it went through some mutations, at least in my brain. At one point, I wanted it to be a monthly, just covering Mississippi. I think that I even thought about doing a weekly paper covering the state or even the town. So it went through all of these shapes and sizes, and I just kept playing around with it and thinking about it. You know, it seemed like such a good, simple idea that it almost seemed too good. I would be asking people for their opinion on it, and everybody pretty much thought it was a good idea.

I still kept holding back on doing anything about it because I felt that I wasn't necessarily ready. I hadn't read enough. Period. I thought that was a big drawback. I thought that I should be more well-rounded before I jumped into something like this. I certainly didn't know grammar rules by heart. I hadn't read all of Faulkner, or any of that sort of thing.

But finally, I just decided that if I didn't do it, someone else would—possibly someone even less qualified than I. So I just started writing to authors whom I liked, and told them what I was doing. I wanted to see if they bought into the idea like some of the other people around me. As it turned out, they did.

I think the turning point was when I got something from John Updike. He sent in a submission, and then I knew that it was going to work. I knew there wasn't any writer worth his or her beans who would not want to be in the magazine with an original John Updike contribution.

At that point, the magazine wasn't solely southern. It was just going to be based in the South and would publish whatever I thought was good.

How did you come up with the money to launch?

I think it cost about ten thousand bucks to print up, and working on a bookstore salary, I, of course, didn't have that and literally had nothing in the bank. Well, almost literally. I'm sure I had about thirty or forty bucks.

So I got my then-roommate's parents to cosign a $6,000 loan, and I raised about $4,000 more in loans from a few people. That allowed me to pay the printing bill.

All the contributors turned down being paid for their work. I think that, originally, I could only offer them about $35, and, after a while, everybody just turned that down. Finally, it was just a case of everybody donating work to the first issue. That was another sign of how much something like this was needed from the South. Here were these great, very busy, very talented people who felt strongly enough about this thing to donate their work.

Look at the John Grisham example. At that time, *The Firm* had just come out, and he was a big hit, and he could have sold his original article to anyone in America for as much as he wanted. But he gave it to us. That sort of signified to me that the whole thing should work.

So from 1992 until John Grisham pumped some blood into this thing, when he became publisher, the magazine said "The Magazine from the South" on the cover. This meant that we would publish stuff that wasn't necessarily southern, just like the *New Yorker* publishes stuff that is not necessarily about New York. But when John came aboard, we refocused and decided to make the magazine exclusively about the South.

What problems did you face before John Grisham came aboard as publisher in 1994?

Oh, everything. Absolutely. It wasn't really a one-person show because I had people volunteering intermittently, but I was the only person who was there for the first year and a half, constantly.

So it was sort of a one-man show, and I didn't have any money, and the only way we could print was by finagling. I've almost sort of blacked it out, but I really had to expend so much creativity into figuring out how to keep the phones on and the lights on that I really desired to be in a position where I could just edit and not have to do those types of things.

What sort of things did you do?

Oh gosh, it was like calling up bookstores or ad people and trying to get the money quicker. You spend all of this time trying to pay the basic bills just so you could exist. They can turn the lights off without much of a problem, but they can't turn the phones off. I know the phone went off once, but that's about it.

It was just a constant battle for money because there was literally nobody backing the magazine. Even though it was a low-interest loan investment, after I got that first $10,000 from those wonderful people, the money was gone. The magazine was on its own. I just had to scrap, borrow, and beg.

How did you overcome discouragement?

It *was* very discouraging at times. Well, Ginsberg has a line in one of his poems where he talks about tragedy. When you are without money, all of a sudden, tragedy is reduced to numbers—and that is exactly what it was.

I just hate that stuff. I want to edit a magazine. I don't want to be talking on the phone and trying to come up with ways to deal with all of the creditors. It was just completely draining.

However, I knew that the idea was sound and people I had long respected, all of these writers and what not, believed in it. They believed in it enough to give me great stuff for free. After the first issue, we just paid very low.

I just knew that it had to live because nobody has been able to tell me the South does not deserve a good, general interest magazine. Nobody has knocked the basic idea and nobody can as far as magazine ideas go.

Everybody talks about the southern literary tradition, and we know that that's a reality. Yet there are hundreds of magazines all grouped together in New York, all knocking each other and copying each other. In the South, there is one general interest magazine, and that is the *Oxford American*, so I could never lose faith in the idea even when it would have been tempting to do so.

So you had these problems. How did you sell this idea to John Grisham?

The same way that I sold him the idea of contributing a manuscript to it. He saw that it was a good idea. The South needs a good magazine like this. It needs one and deserves one and, the belief is, can support one. We haven't seen that completely yet, but I still believe it. That's what attracted him to it.

It's also the fact that the standards we have for the kind of writing we accept are pretty high when you compare them nationwide. I don't think that it is as good as the *New Yorker* or the *Atlantic Monthly* or *Harper's* yet, but it's in the top eight maybe as far as publishing great writing.

And that's another reason. I think he thought that it was doing something valuable.

Is flexibility important in launching a magazine?

I think that it is idiotic to go into a situation with preconceptions and then learn that those preconceptions are not exactly accurate and then not change slightly. I had ideas and goals when I started, and I have had to stick to them because that is what I said that I was going to do. But you have to be willing to listen and learn.

Nobody knows everything about everything, and I think that one of the things that makes people great and makes certain magazines great is all of the individual contributions that each person makes. It's like a puzzle, and each person adds his or her contribution to the overall picture. You just can't be an island. You can't do it alone. I think it's absurd to even suggest that you know it all.

What advice would you give someone preparing to launch a magazine?

I guess it would depend on what they were launching. I mean, actually I would not talk, I could not talk to them about, say, a boat motor magazine. I only know literature.

Overall, I guess I would say, "Know what you are doing." You should be passionate about it. All the great editors and all of the great magazines that I look up to seem to have been led and engineered by people who were just loaded down with passion and vision. The *New Yorker*, *Vanity Fair*, the *Atlantic Monthly*, *Harper's*, all of those had people behind them who had high standards, a deep commitment, and a love for what they were doing. That's why those things are special.

When you recruited your staff, what things did you look for and what problems did you see?

Well, first of all, even though John saved us, we are still a very small budget enterprise. We don't make that much money, and we are understaffed and all of that. We are doing our best to change that, but it's a slow process.

But you know, right off the bat that meant that I had to look for people locally, and there were a lot of people for whom it would have been impossible to work for what we were offering. You know, people with a family, people for whom this would be the only income, that sort of thing.

But what I looked for in these people was pretty much what I looked for in myself. That is, I wanted these people to be passionate and intelligent, and I wanted them to be able to see things for themselves, and feel like we are all in a position where we can create things. We were and still are in a position to define things, and I want people who can create and make it better.

At the time, I was looking for, and I guess I still am looking for, people who can bring things to the magazine that I don't bring—people who can stretch me, too. I don't want to be the one who comes up with all of the ideas. I wouldn't want somebody in here who just had worked in a magazine before and just knew one way of doing things because that wouldn't necessarily work for us. We needed to be flexible because we wanted to do new things. How can you be inflexible and do new things?

But I'm not interested in people's resumés or grade point averages. I didn't go to college myself, so it's not something that I necessarily put a lot of stock into. I was just looking for people whom I thought would bring something dangerously near visionary to the magazine. People who wouldn't just bring life and blood and all of that, but folks who were also committed to getting it done, no matter how long it took.

With a small run magazine where people have so many different duties, we don't have the luxury of just reading manuscripts or whatever. You really don't know what you have as far as folks go until they are in the office. If somebody calls me up and says they know someone who would be great for this magazine, that doesn't mean anything to me. I've learned, in some ways, that the people here do a little bit of everything—probably more than any other place that I have heard of because the place is small. Nobody specializes in any one department. From PR campaigns, to advertising, to circulation—we all have to do everything.

You learn quickly who can do what. I have only hired one person who had previous magazine experience out of the ten or twelve who have gone through our doors.

Is lack of sufficient funding the biggest problem you have faced so far?

For this particular magazine, yes, I think so. Looking over our history, I think that may have been the most trying thing.

That, and personnel problems. They have been trying, too. I have learned that I am not the easiest person to work with. I am pretty set on where we should go. I don't know where or how, but I know that we have got to be one of the better magazines in the country as far as what we are doing, and that is easier said than done. And so I like to say that I have high standards. I am sure that people who have been unhappy with me as their boss would view it differently. They would say that I am cold or unkind or whatever, but those would be the two biggest problems for this particular enterprise.

Some magazines are well-funded, and I am sure that some have very few personnel problems, and some magazines are among the best in the country. I would love to be a fly on the wall and see how many magazines fit in all three categories. It would be great, but we certainly aren't there yet. We are not in all three categories, but we're working on it.

NOTES

· ·

· ·

· ·

· ·

· ·

· ·

· ·

· ·

· ·

· ·

· ·

· ·

· ·

· ·

· ·

· ·

· ·

By now, you should have an excellent grasp of your magazine's personality. You've planted the concept in the minds of enough people to know typical reader behavior when confronted with hypothetical situations. Your baby's been tested, tweaked, and is ready to be subjected to the rigors of strategic positioning in the marketplace.

CIRCULATION

9

If you've run to the grocery store for coffee and toilet paper, does the latest issue of *Shoelace Monthly* constitute a substantial enough draw to get you to leave the snack aisle? Would you rather not be seen purchasing it, preferring, rather, to have it sent to your mailbox (in a plain, brown wrapper)? Does the thought of being able to purchase *Modern Cuticle* only at manicurists' shops somehow make it more appealing, as though you were a member of an exclusive club?

THE CIRCULATION PLAN

These are questions you should address in your circulation plan. They also constitute the three ways you have at your disposal as you force your publication into the hands of the public. That is, you can distribute via single-copy sales (the traditional newsstand), direct mail (subscriptions), or alternate routes (specialty retail outlets or other nontraditional racks). It is your job as the clever upstart to decide where you'll strike first and hardest.

Pavlov Knows Best

But before you go piling your publication onto every

newsstand in sight, you should let old Pavlov give your content the once-over. It is essential to understand that established magazines are purchased either on impulse or by habit.

Not every magazine with a circulation of a million is an automatic sell-out. Some magazines must maintain a level of either celebrity or cleavage on the cover in order to move off the shelf.

Not every magazine with a circulation of a million is an automatic sell-out. Some magazines must maintain a level of either celebrity or cleavage on the cover in order to move off the shelf. That makes it an impulse buy. If the celebrity of the minute is on the cover, it's a big seller. Or, if some model strikes a particularly seductive or revealing pose, it's a big seller. This is why *People Weekly* has far more than a million copies in weekly single-copy sales. They understand their content. They know they live and die by the cult of celebrity, and every week they call that spade a spade. In so doing, they consistently sell 3.5 million copies.

The other publications must rely on reader loyalty. Like Pavlov's slobbering mongrel, the behavior of many readers has been fully conditioned. In other words, most readers have at least one favorite magazine that they will purchase regardless of who graces the cover. The magazine hits the newsstand, they make a purchase. It makes no difference if it's Claudia, Paulina, Cindy, or Naomi on the cover, hundreds of thousands of readers will pick up *Cosmo* every month. Same thing with *Rolling Stone*, same thing with *Playboy*.

Newsstand Darwinism

How is your magazine received? If you feel you can generate habitual behavior, you can count on higher subscriptions than newsstand sales. If not, then place an obscene amount of weight on your cover designs. In fact, plan on that right from the start. The newsstand has always been and will always be the acid test for any new magazine. Technology may have splintered distribution down a number of new avenues with CD-ROMs and the Web, but the newsstand is where it is inexorably based.

Detractors of the newsstand say it is too crowded, and new magazines will undoubtedly be lost in the shuffle. Wrong! If your competitor is on the newsstand, then *you* must be on the newsstand. You must be right next to it, offering a viable alternative to what is already out there.

Let newsstand Darwinism decide who survives. Running away to hide will get you nowhere but out of mind.

Conversely, if your competitor is not on the newsstand, ask yourself why. Use old-fashioned common sense when assessing your distribution options.

THE JOURNEY BEGINS

Launching a magazine would be a no-brain, cash-soaked venture were it not for the network of distributors, wholesalers, and retailers. Getting your magazine from the printer to the newsstand is a bit like the adage that says making law is like making sausage—the finished product is fine, as long as you don't witness its creation.

Launching a magazine would be a no-brain, cash-soaked venture were it not for the national network of distributors, wholesalers, and retailers.

The long road a magazine must hoe begins when the publisher sends the designs to the printer. The printer works his magic and your baby is born, stapled, and stacked in the corner of a warehouse. From there, you must rely on the kindness of strangers.

Distributors

The first key player is your distributor. Before printing, you must work up a deal with one of seven major distributors or one of twenty smaller ones. These companies serve dual, vital roles for your publication. Not only are they responsible for overseeing the delivery and marketing of your magazine in the marketplace, but they also serve as a money collector between you and the next key player: the wholesaler.

Wholesalers

The wholesaler's job is to receive the magazines directly from the printer and to perform the actual delivery to the predetermined newsstands. Currently, there are between sixty and sixty-five wholesalers around the country, each with a specific territory into which no other wholesaler may enter. The wholesaler collects the cash from the retailer and picks up the sales records and the unsold copies. The unsold copies are run through the paper shredder and the cash is sent to the distributor.

The Numbers

This sounds easy enough, until you see the numbers. Remember, newsstand sales hover around the 40% mark. Out of every 100 magazines you print for the newsstand, you sell 40. Of that 40% sell-through, retailers claim between 20% and 30%, wholesalers grab 20% to 25%, and distributors take about 10%. So the total distribution process eats up about 60% of sales profit. What's worse, you don't see a dime of that newsstand profit for nearly 6 months after the point of sale!

Out of every 100 magazines you print for the newsstand, you sell 40. Of that 40% sell-through, retailers claim between 20% and 30%, wholesalers grab 20% to 25%, and distributors take about 10%.

Worse still, the whole ordeal is based on trust. Because the magazine trade is all done on consignment, you must trust your distributor to market your magazine properly, you must trust the wholesaler to record the numbers accurately, and you must trust the retail outlet to sell what is available to sell.

As you might guess, every step of the way is ripe for fraud. Because records are kept by scanning bar codes, ripping the bar code from a magazine cover and reporting it as unsold is an incredibly easy way for unseemly characters to rip off magazine publishers. In essence, the door is wide open for freeloading folks to get magazines at the publisher's expense, because he or she never sees the unsold product.

Distributors to the Rescue

This may sound like more trouble than it's worth, but it is a very efficient system. For instance, *TV Guide* prints on a Sunday, gets to wholesalers around 3 A.M. Monday, and hits newsstands across America by daybreak. In order to achieve this level of efficiency for your venture, you must get the best distributor for your needs.

Think of your distributor as your agent. Like a Hollywood talent agent, your distributor represents your magazine in the marketplace of opportunities. The distributor will know where your publication should be displayed and has the marketing know-how to get it there, and serves as a liaison between you and the hundreds of wholesalers out there. Can you imagine coordinating the delivery of 150,000 magazines to 200 wholesalers who lay it on 20,000 newsstands? You need the distributor to do this tedious work.

Retail Display Allowance

It doesn't take Sherlock Holmes to notice that some magazines get better newsstand real estate than others. Some are fully exposed on the front row, others are tucked away on row five such that only the top three inches are in view. Still others get their own suite of space next to the cash register. What gives?

Well, your wallet, for starters. This placement of titles owes primarily to the Retail Display Allowance, or R.D.A. It's what a magazine publisher pays a retailer for favorable placement.

Pockets

Currently, your typical R.D.A. is about 10% above what the retailer already charges. That will get you special placement on the newsstand. The really special placement comes when you rent a "pocket." Pockets are the rack locations separate from the "mainline" (the regular newsstand). In a grocery store, it's on the check-out line. In most places, it's next to the cash register for those point-of-purchase sales.

Pocket rental can cost up to $25 extra per month. That doesn't seem like much when your printing costs hit the $100,000 mark and ad revenue isn't far behind, but think about how many retail outlets there are. Then think about how many magazines you could sell in a good pocket, multiply it by the cover price, subtract the standard R.D.A., then subtract the additional $25. Does it make financial sense to be there?

In some cases, yes, it makes perfect sense. Strategically, you can think of this pocket as a billboard. It's practically a direct mail campaign where people can pick up and sample your product and decide, first, if they want to buy it, and, second, if they want to subscribe to it. If the weather forecast calls for a clear, beautiful weekend, grocery carts will overflow with food for parties and cookouts. Thus, the wait in line will be so long that people may

Can you imagine coordinating the delivery of 150,000 magazines to 200 wholesalers who lay it on 20,000 newsstands? You need the distributor to do this tedious work.

spend more time reading your magazine at the check-out counter than in their own living room. It's practically a captive audience!

This R.D.A. and pocket rental conundrum is one issue your distributor irons out with you. Once you decide you can afford something of that nature, the distributor finds the best deals. These fees are negotiable. Remember, Jim Carrey didn't always earn $20 million per film. He made one blockbuster, and then let his agent go to work.

Nontraditional Distributors

What I've been describing so far is the traditional distribution set-up. A single national distributor represents your magazine, determines where it should be placed, and tells the printer how many copies to send to which whole-salers. It's expensive, but the power and effectiveness of this time-proven network excuse most of the headaches it may cause.

However, ambitious niche publications now have an alternative. In recent years, a new breed of distributors has emerged. These nontraditional, independent distributors are bypassing wholesalers and placing the magazines on the racks themselves.

In recent years, a new breed of distributors has emerged. Nontraditional, independent distributors are bypassing wholesalers and placing the magazines on the racks themselves.

But not just any magazine racks. Not only do they handle magazines with a shorter press run than the traditional distributors would accept, but they also pinpoint specific specialty locations at which to place the publications. In other words, nontraditional distributors use a relatively low number of "smart bombs," whereas the traditionals bring in a fleet of B-52's for some good old-fashioned carpet bombing.

For instance, if you're launching a magazine called *Cabinets and Kitchen Sinks*, you don't want to throw 20,000 copies away at every Wal-Mart on the continent. You'll want a specific number delivered to hand-picked home supply and design stores. This is where the independent distributors help you out.

And don't fret about gaping holes on the wholesale delivery end. Many of these distributors work together by forming a network so they can outsource their national delivery. In a nutshell, the printer ships the entire press run to, say, Chicago (assuming that's where your distributor is located). This distributor then decides which of the other independent distributors will be needed to fulfill the circulation plan and promptly ships the correctly sized bundles to the proper companies.

The end result is niche distribution. And in this age of niche magazine launches, you can infer which school of distribution is growing fastest.

DIRECT MAIL

If this distributor/wholesaler/retailer game doesn't sound appealing to you, there is an alternative. Direct mail campaigns may be able to help you navigate around the newsstand by moving directly into people's homes.

Though you won't launch with tens of thousands of subscribers, a solid subscription base can be built early in the proceedings. With mature publications, 23% of sales are from the newsstand, while the remaining 77% go to subscribers. With a freshman publication, the numbers are exactly opposite. Your goal, then, is to build, build, build your direct mail sales.

Remember, you only sell about 40% of what you put on the rack. That's a printing waste of 60%. With subscriptions, you waste nothing. And, the money is paid up front. So, how do you get the percentages to flip-flop in your favor?

With mature publications, 23% of sales are from the newsstand, while the remaining 77% go to subscribers. With a freshman publication, the numbers are exactly opposite.

The Package

Good direct mail packages are an art revered by magazine publishers and hated by everyone else. It boosts the bottom line at magazines, but clutters up the mailbox of Joe Citizen. It's junk mail, plain and simple. You are constructing an envelope of goodies that asks for money from somebody already irritated by credit card debt and mortgage payments. They hold bills in one hand, and your marketing savvy in the other. So you better make it good. It's your bread and butter.

To this end, there are five key components to every worthwhile direct mail packet.

1. The Letter

You must write a sparkling, painless letter of invitation to prospective subscribers. Make it as detailed as possible. Don't take them for fools if they're putting checks in the mail. They're going to want to know what they're getting into. Explain your concept, then explain it again. Let loose the same passion you unloaded on your investors. To a billionaire, a couple of million bucks of venture capital for a magazine launch requires a modicum of thought. Same thing for the middle-class magazine reader and his twenty-dollar subscription.

Throw in some psychological appeal. Tell your targets how the magazine will make their lives better. It will brighten their days and keep them informed! Don't lie, but don't be too humble, either.

Also, let them in on your special offer. It's an introductory rate, it's only available for charter subscribers, everybody gets a free pair of pants! Something to that effect. Remember, you're selling a magazine that doesn't exist to people who don't have money to burn. Read that sentence again. So you need to make potential subscribers feel special. Make them feel like they're getting the deal of a lifetime.

> **Remember, you're selling a magazine that doesn't exist to people who don't have money to burn. Make them feel special. Make them feel like they're getting the deal of a lifetime.**

Specifically, the elements you should include in your letter are the concept, the audience you aim to serve, your offer, the contents of the magazine, and the relationship of this magazine to the subject matter and to the audience. In other words, what relationship does this publication have to reality? Why must it happen now, and why must these individuals be involved?

2. The Poster

Throw a sample poster into the packet. Compile a couple of your best layouts on a full-color page to let them know what they'll be receiving every month. Show them a cover design. Show them a department. You'd be surprised at the number of people who will buy a magazine simply because it looks hip or fresh or otherwise current. Make sure this poster reflects that. If it looks as if a second-grader designed it, it will be ignored.

3. The Testimonial

For an added dose of psychology, convince an authority or expert in the field your magazine covers to write a "Lift-up Letter." It should be a 5x7 note written by this individual for the purpose of assuring the unconvinced subscribers-to-be that they have nothing to lose. In fact, they can cancel at any time with no further obligation!

Then turn up the heat. Have your expert say that, frankly, they'd be surprised if the readers did not subscribe. There's no reason to say no. In other words, apply the psychological pressure to help motivate the sale.

4. The Response Card

Now for the fun part. You've got to make the response card as easy as possible, yet as intriguing and interactive as possible at the same time. This gets tricky because you only have about twenty-five square inches in which to play. Though this prevents you from asking potential customers to write a book for you, it also cuts down on the layout possibilities. So be clever rather than artistic.

Make the subscribers-to-be tear something off or plant a sticker in a "savings zone." Without being too goofy, give it a gimmick or a joke. Obviously, *Mad* magazine would tell a different joke than would *Esquire*, so tread lightly. Some magazines shouldn't tell a joke at all. How many new subscribers would the *Economist* get if it began its card with "How many mutual fund managers does it take to screw in a light bulb?" Not too many, and certainly not the right kind.

5. The Envelope, Please

The envelope is as crucial as the cover of your magazine on the crowded newsstand. How many times have you tossed unopened, direct mail pieces directly into the trash? A lot! Why? Probably because you took one look at it and thought, "This is somebody asking me for money, and it doesn't look like I'll get anything in return." Even Ed McMahon's promises of great wealth don't convince most people to open their sweepstakes envelopes.

With this in mind, you've got to construct an "Open Me!" envelope. It's got to scream. Use the right colors and fonts. If you think most envelopes are garish and ugly, make yours simple and classy. If you think nobody opens direct mail, make the envelope look like a bill. When they open it and see that it's not, they'll be relieved. But never, never, never deceive or irritate your targets. Rather, you must intrigue and entice. The key point is this: If your direct mail doesn't begin with a knock-out envelope, everything else is a waste.

6. Getting It There

Of course, the perfect direct mail package is worthless if it's sent to the wrong people. You've got to rent a list of names or a database from a list broker. This broker will supply you with a custom designed batch of names and addresses to fit your audience description.

If your direct mail doesn't begin with a knock-out envelope, everything else is a waste.

Don't get carried away with volume. Each name may seem cheap (between 8¢ and 10¢ each), but you can throw away thousands of dollars in the blink of an eye if you don't pay attention. It's far more complex than just thumbing through the phone book. If you're launching *Media Mogul Illustrated*, you may want to rent a list of television and radio station owners in America. If you're launching *Hunting Aficionado*, avoid the People for the Ethical Treatment of Animals membership list. You get the point.

CONCLUSION

As you map out your circulation strategy, always keep your magazine's concept and audience in mind. It may look easy on the surface—you design it and it ends up on the newsstand—but dodging the bullets along the way can make or break your publication. Make wise marketing decisions, especially when choosing your distributor.

Do this and you'll be head and shoulders above the rest.

John Mack Carter is president of Hearst Magazines Enterprises, and Tom O'Neil is editorial director. Hearst Magazines Enterprises was founded in 1995 as an entity to help launch new magazines.

Interview:

John Mack Carter & Tom O'Neil
Hearst Magazines Enterprises

What's the difference between the magazine of the '90s, of the '50s, and of 1741, when the first magazine was launched?

Carter: The magazine of the '90s is coming around to be more like the magazine of 1741 than in any of the intervening periods. Between then and now, magazines went through the full period of developing this relationship between editor and reader to its fullest, and, in building this network, built magazines as a national media.

That is what builds magazines as a national media, and because of that success, magazines became a great advertising force. The success that magazines have had with advertising made it big business. And in the process of becoming successful with big businesses, that relationship between the editor and reader sometimes was clouded. It was not as clear.

The first time I sat in Harvard and listened to a case history on magazines, the instructor started out with a question, "What is the purpose of magazine publishing?" And I was sitting there thinking, "To make a better world and to leave a person better educated." I got through with all the things I had listed and his answer was one I had not listed. His answer was, "To make money."

I understand that as one of the purposes, but as *the* purpose, at the time, came as a surprise. But it's always been an underlying purpose. I figure that making money, basically, is what you do to enable you to carry out your other purposes of the magazine. The two almost always go hand in hand because, without making money, you are not going to do the good that you can do and be that cultural and societal force that a magazine can be. But I think what has happened, even having had an industrial and a technological revolution, we are not any smarter and we are not any better informed or better motivated than we were when the first magazine came out 250 years ago.

What we are is better equipped to retain elements of individuality. We are much better equipped to do it than when magazine publishing involved millions of everything— millions of staples, millions of tons of paper, tons of ink, and millions of problems. Whereas now, the editor can carry the process of publishing to the reader in a much more personal manner than any time since 1741. That is, the editor can carry on with the planning and the writing and take it right to the point of printing, actually moving into the press room through the computer and electronic publishing. So that is the big difference.

The other big difference is, I remember, when I was chief editor of *McCall's*. In 1963 we hit 8 million circulation. At that time, it was the biggest magazine with the exception of *Reader's Digest*. I think it was bigger at that time than *TV Guide* was. There was a lunch given in celebration and a little trophy was up here at the office, and it was engraved "8 million," and it had underneath there "1960—7 million" and "1963—8 million," then "10 million" and a question mark or blank to be filled in.

The drive was for circulation. The bigger the magazine, the better. That was the problem with *Look*, *Life*, and *Saturday Evening Post*. They were fighting for total circulation, figuring whoever had the biggest total circulation was going to win. That was true in those days. That question mark on *McCall's* was never filled in with a date because it never reached 10 million. It reached 8½ million and then started going down. Today, it has 5 million circulation.

This does not mean total circulation has nothing to do with success; it has to do with the change in the purpose of magazines and the change in the publishing philosophy and economic realities of magazine publishing. Now, instead of the biggest circulation, you have the ideal of getting the purest circulation—the smaller the number you can have and still dominate a field. That is the ideal circulation.

Today we see more circulation driven magazines, with less dependency on advertising. Is it because of an advertising depression, or is it a trend?

Carter: Neither. It's because when advertising becomes hard to sell, most of us explain the deficiency by saying we have "changed our minds—we are not looking for it— what we really want is circulation success." In truth, we want both and we need both.

Can you differentiate between the service journalism magazines and the nonservice? What is your definition of service journalism?

Carter: Service journalism is journalism that has the goal and the discipline of instruction—instruction on making things, on doing things. It primarily deals with that which can be touched and seen as opposed to the journalism that deals with concepts and thoughts.

You were once quoted as saying that newsstand or single-copy sales were the acid test for any new magazine. That was fifteen years ago. Do you still believe that?

Carter: I still believe it, and the difference between now and then is the acid bath is a lot more bitter and vitriolic than it was then. It does not take as long to succumb to the acid as it used to take. But it is still the test.

The problem today is that the newsstand is a democratic operation. The way the distribution to the newsstands is set up rewards the broadest possible distribution interest. It reaches the common denominator in a broad way and not in a specific way. It is not designed, and still does not function, selectively on an audience.

Where most new magazines today need to be a special interest or selective publication, it is not impossible or inefficient to use the general newsstand to market a special interest or a selective publication. So you can still use it as a test, and I do, but the scores are different. You cannot expect the same scores. As long as you change the scorecard, you can still use the test.

You have probably launched more magazines in your career than any other person I can think of. Can you take us through the steps of what happens after the idea is born?

Carter: Well, most good magazine ideas are not precise. They are ideas that lend themselves to others. They are like a glob of Silly Putty. There is something in there that can be shaped into exactly what you want, but it is not there when it starts out. But you know when you feel it that it has some value. You know, when you work it around in the mind, what it should sound like, feel like, and look like.

That just takes place in the mind. You decide what the validity of an idea is all by yourself. As I say, an idea is just a glob of putty. It has to be worked on, and it can be brainstormed, but it cannot be group managed. It has to be a single individual listening to everybody, then shaping that idea, that putty, into the form he or she wants.

I'll get ideas from the newspaper, from some demographic, or, more likely, from some political issue. Once, when I was coming back from London during an election period, I found the Green Party had scored a significant number of votes, a good 20% of the votes in this election. I realized that this type of protest vote was something that was happening over there while nothing was happening in this country.

Earth Day was then splashed on the front pages and disappeared. And it hit me on the plane flying back that the movement was still here, but had no voice and was not being treated in any way outside the special interest groups. There was no broad treatment of the fact that the people were ready to respond to the environment and to the dangers of their own lives. It wasn't from a health standpoint as much as from the standpoint that they were losing something valuable for their children.

So out of that conviction, I thought it through. I noticed there were a lot of publishers around who were developing large-format magazines, which were being successfully sold. They were also using very high-quality physical products in a small circulation run, so I began assembling the specific elements for that kind of publication. The elements being ripping out photographs, tear sheets, something I saw in a book or magazine—anything from my own experience—over a period of a month.

I shaped this into a loose-leaf dummy, just by throwing ideas in. I was not trying to define it with words at all, but instead I was thinking it through based on my experience of what a profitable circulation level might be. Generally, I wanted to know whether there would be enough support for that type of magazine—what kind of advertiser it would take, and so forth.

I'm not really trying to shop it around just yet, but I take it on the basis of prior activity and success, and I go to the president of the company and say, "Here is a magazine that I want to do." The president, who spends most of his time looking at one-hundred-page legal documents and contracts and a lot of other kinds of research, finds it refreshing just to be talking about something else. He is able to come up with a simple response. That response being, "O.K., let's do it."

From there, I call on magazine development, which is a freelance operation. So the editor of magazine development and I begin writing words down for subject matter—for features, for columns—and then we go to other people and come back with a list of column ideas and maybe even writers. Then we begin to put together tables of content and try to put together about six issues.

Then I call on the advertising department to come up with a corporate ad department for the publication. They begin researching the market, like who the advertisers will be. And they begin writing the marketing position for the publication.

I call the people who are responsible for the newsstand

distribution and for subscriptions together—the top people who give me advice—and ask them what they think. This goes on for several meetings and it is up to them to determine how many copies they want to put out.

The subscription numbers are set so they can get started thinking about how many of our other magazine readers might be approached successfully by this magazine. How many readers of *Town & Country* could be converted into readers of this new magazine I'm calling *Countryside*? How many readers of *Victoria* could be converted to *Countryside*?

Then we go for the time all this should go on the market. We pick a circulation date—we want to go on the newsstand on October 15. Then we give that figure to the production department. That is the mechanical department of the company, which says that there are certain printers we can approach. We have space available. Schedule the prepress and get back down to scheduling for when we go to the newsstand.

They tell me when we have to go to press and when the last page has to close, when things are due at the engraver, when composition has to be done, and all the way down to the magazine development editor saying how long it is going to take to do the editing—about thirty days.

Then we have a D-day for when we actually start. From there, we go back to the president—all of us do, everybody he might want to hear from—and say, "Here is the proposition." Meanwhile, the financial manager has done a pro forma based on the assumptions I have given him—the number of editorial pages, the number of advertising pages expected, the anticipated sales at the newsstands, and all the expenses. He does a pro forma on what it is going to cost. From that, we seek approval to go ahead. Approval may be given or the proposal may be sent back for another seven days to get more information.

What are you trying to test when you put a magazine on the stands with more than one cover or with different cover prices in different areas?

Carter: We determine that this magazine is going to have a $2.95 cover price. That is what it ought to be because of the other magazines of that quality.

But the purpose of this first magazine is to get it into as many hands as possible. So, instead of the $2.95, we may elect to put it out at $1.95 to increase the sale. But the $1.95 is not a realistic price for a commercial title. It is not what we want. We will want to sell it later on for $2.95. So, as long as we are already going out, we will put out a small number at $2.95 to see what the difference in sales is. That enables us to make other projections concerning profitability down the line. We're just trying to learn a lot of information from very little effort.

And what about the different cover photographs?

Carter: *Countryside* is an example because the question is whether it is an emotional appeal and, therefore, the picture should be one that conjures up children, the rewards of growing up in the countryside, as opposed to a photograph of specific people who are living in the countryside. One is evocative while the other is more of a news magazine approach, a more direct approach to, say, picture this family or this person or this couple.

See, we're just testing the cover, not the magazine. But I learn something dramatic from it. It is just a hedge to keep from having some bad surprises later on. It's an opportunity, at almost no cost, to learn one more thing.

Some of the magazines you have tested are tested as spin-offs, like *Country Living*, *Countryside*, and *Good Housekeeping's Victoria*. Is that for the sake of name recognition?

Carter: Two things. *Country Living* was originally *Good Housekeeping's Country Living*. It is always a pattern because of the importance of the newsstand. Its reputation is accepted in supermarkets everywhere. Anything that *Good Housekeeping* publishes as a cooking magazine or decorating magazine is also automatically accepted because people know it will not be pornographic. It will have a certain quality, a good value.

If I am trying to get a magazine at eight thousand supermarkets, rather than having somebody make the call and start selling this new magazine, I can say it is *Good Housekeeping's Country Living*. Then it becomes much more automatic for them to accept it and give it display at the newsstand. That is the primary thing.

And the other is to identify the heritage for the reader. As in other things in life, the best way to identify a child is by having the last name be the same as the parents'.

Let's jump forward to the year 2001. Do you see any difference in the magazines on the market?

Carter: I think by the year 2001, we will have as many magazines as we have now, but I do not think we will have a greater total circulation. I think we will have fewer magazines to choose from on the newsstand because the newsstand will be a more efficient operation. There will be a self-policing policy at newsstands. Instead of wasting more than 50% of all this paper and effort going to the newsstands, we'll just reduce the waste. There will be fewer newsstands, fewer copies accepted for newsstand distribution, and those that make it will be better displayed and better sold and, therefore, far more commercially efficient than they are today.

This merely means that magazines will mostly be distributed by private distribution organizations and private mail services that will be owned by a combination of the publishers and printers. Most of the circulation will be handled by direct delivery. There will still be a few magazines of large circulation, of multi-million circulation, but not as many as there are today.

When should direct mail testing begin?

Carter: Not in the first phase. Involve the magazine staff so they can begin writing and thinking. Direct mail comes in the second phase, after we get it going. It is so expensive and slow that there is no use in doing it until we are sure. We are interested, first, in the magazine. Then we can go out and run a mail test.

What are some qualities that cause a magazine idea to be rejected?

O'Neil: It can be a great idea but just not a Hearst idea. That is the hardest part of my job—turning down ideas that are actually wonderful, but that just don't fit into our corporate picture.

How many magazines get the green light?

O'Neil: We test two or three new concepts every year.

And you see close to three hundred?

O'Neil: Right.

So about 1% actually make it?

O'Neil: Yeah, but with the titles that we are testing now, none came from people sending them to us. We should not discourage them from doing that in the future.

Bob Vila's American Home came as a result of our discussions with Bob over the years about doing such a magazine. *Healthy Living*, which is being tested under the monarch of *Country Living*, deals with homeopathic medicine and health treatments. That happens to be the passion of *Country Living* editor-in-chief Rachel Newman.

Now we are doing another new magazine called *Mr. Food's Easy Cooking*. And Mr. Food is one of the best selling cookbook authors at Hearst's book division, William Morrow. So we saw his huge sales numbers over there and said, well, maybe this is a magazine, too. Let's give it a shot. But we are still looking through the mail every day for that diamond in the rough.

Are there any ideas that haven't been explored?

O'Neil: Oh sure, many of them. Whether or not they are good ideas is still to be decided.

Have you ever believed in a concept, supported it fully, only to have it fail in the long run?

O'Neil: Oh, yeah. I've seen many very good ideas that we just couldn't do here because they didn't fit. One very good example is a magazine coming out of Chicago now called *Modern Dad*. That just strikes me as a natural parenting title.

Whom do I expect will do well in the long run? In many cases these have to be hatched as home magazines first, before big capitals or big publishing companies come behind them.

Now that you know the basics about your magazine, it's time to start assembling a staff. How many people will it take to churn out your baby? Who will be in charge of what? How can you possibly turn a profit while paying salaries and benefits?

THE STAFF 10

Let's start from the top.

Unless you are born into a media mogul's family, or your rich uncle happens to own a newspaper or a television or radio station and he decides to bequeath it to you rather than to his own kids, chances are slim you'll be launching one of these media ventures. The amount of capital needed to get a television station off the ground is obscene. Ever shopped for a printing press? They ain't free.

Magazines, on the other hand, are cheap. Well, cheap in the sense that your last name doesn't have to be Hearst, Buffett, Turner, or Gannett to launch one. You're your own boss right from the get-go. No corporate ladder climbing or serving as vice-president-in-charge-of-coffee-cream-and-two-sugars.

That's why there are more magazines than any other form of media. And that's why there are more entrepreneurs in the magazine industry, more folks doing it for themselves, than in any other form of media.

What is an entrepreneur? It's a person who takes a calculated risk on a venture in which he or she hopes to make a pile of cash. Remember, magazines are for making money. It is a business, not a charity. You may wish to make Joe Reader happy, but if you aren't returning on your investors' capital, they cut the purse strings.

After *Tribe* magazine, based in New Orleans, hit its one-year mark, the publisher asked me to drop in for a visit and a check-up. They had already spent half a million clams in twelve months, and their investor said he needs to be convinced of the need to blow another half a million for year two. Will he ever get his money back? What does the future look like?

So I polished my biggest crystal ball, called a psychic hot-line, and rolled into the Big Easy.

Get my point? If you call yourself the publisher, you must be a gutsy entrepreneur as well. It is not enough simply to love magazines in order to enter this business. You must be painfully aware that you and your investors could lose your shirts. But, in magazine utopia, you could do well enough to buy stock in Brooks Brothers. It can go either way, and it is your job as publisher, at the top of the staff food chain, to decide how to calculate that risk and how to execute all of the necessary strategies.

It is not enough simply to love magazines in order to go into this business. You must be painfully aware that you and your investors could lose your shirts.

But how many people must you draw into your tangled web? What are the bare bones of staffing?

Less Is More

Even major companies like the Meredith Corporation, which publishes *Better Homes and Gardens* (among others), use a small staff for start-ups. When they launched *Midwest Living*, they used a full-time staff of seven people. Here's one of the largest media conglomerates in the country, and they launch with seven staff members! When *Golf for Women* launched from Oxford, Mississippi, they only had a staff of four. In fact, a national magazine with a circulation of 50,000, 75,000, or even 100,000 may have a smaller staff than that of a small-town, weekly newspaper with a circulation of 5,000. Amazing, but true. It doesn't take many people to produce a magazine.

This being said, I must remind you that the smaller the staff, the bigger your workload. Duh! Seriously, if you try to scrimp and save on salaries and staff size, you may see less daylight, put a strain on your marriage, and sprout ulcers like a Dalmatian has spots. Thus, love your magazine. Treat it like a friend you choose to spend time with rather than like a job, like a daily grind. Chances are, you're starting this publication to escape the daily grind of your last job anyway.

You need to create an atmosphere for your staff that's the opposite of, "OK, here's my time card. I punch in at 8 A.M., take an hour lunch, then punch out at 5 P.M." Trust me, you won't be spending 8-to-5 hours at this job. You could work 16-hour days, maybe even pull an all-nighter if you're not ready for deadline. And you won't get paid for these extra hours, either. You're working for your baby, not for your paycheck.

Egomania

Which brings me to the next point. Being a magazine publisher and/or editor is likely the most egoistic position in any industry. The pride that swells in your gut when you see your name as "Publisher/Editor" at the top of the masthead is knee-buckling. When you flip through those pages—black and white, color, it doesn't matter—you'll eventually get to your photo at the top of the Letter from the Editor. You can show it to the stranger next to you at the magazine rack and say, "Hey, this is my magazine. Look at me, this is me on this page. I did this. It's mine."

How many newspaper editors have their photo next to their column? None. They're not allowed to. Their opinion is supposed to be the consensus opinion of the entire publication and, as such, is not singled out as the voice of any single person. Magazines are an entirely different ego trip. Not only does the editor get a photo, but most also include a signature, as though it were an actual, personal letter to the reader. Does this make it more personal? Not necessarily. Does it help make the editor a celebrity? You betcha.

So how many people does this editor need to help him or her run the show? Well, in every magazine, there are two sides: business and editorial. You've got to have folks to mind the money and folks to actually create the magazine. In the good old days, the two sides were separated like

Magazines are an entirely different ego trip. Not only does the editor get a photo, but most now include a signature, as though it were an actual, personal letter to the reader.

church and state. Now, it's a mercuric line. Staff members usually need to hop the fence to see how to do their job. Editorial content directs ad sales, graphic design must fit the content like a glove, and ads should reflect the feel of the overall design style. Obviously, you're going to need wide hallways or a good e-mail system in your office to accommodate all the necessary communication between departments.

Or, you'll just need a clear head. With a new magazine, you'll often find that the publisher who runs the business side and the editor who runs the creative side are the same person—you.

Publisher

If you had to choose the most important staff member, it would definitely be the publisher. The publisher is the strong-arm in charge of the budget, from drawing it up to maintaining it. He or she oversees every single expenditure, from salaries, to editorial expenses, to printing costs, to media kit production. The publisher also has to make sure that all revenues due the magazine end up in the bank. Further, it is mainly this person's job to make waves in the industry in order to draw in advertisers and media attention.

Advertising Director

The publisher may have an advertising director to assist in the day-to-day work of generating ad revenue. He or she would be second in command, and would handle follow-up calls, meetings, presentations, you name it, in the name of advertising. I hate to say that ad directors do the grunt work, but that's essentially it. They do what the publisher does not have time to wrestle with. The ad director's plans are then carried out by the sales staff.

Circulation Director

Also reporting to the publisher on the business side is the circulation director. This staff member is in charge of the distribution of the magazine, the actual nuts and bolts of getting it into the readers' hands. Just remember that the circulation director may be assisted by a single-copy manager, who makes sure the magazine arrives on the news-stands as intended, and the direct mail manager, who follows the subscription side of circulation.

So, to reduce this to a flowchart, you have the publisher at the top, then the ad director, the circulation director, and the editor on the second tier. Like I said above, there should be a bridge between each of these second-level positions. Just because they report directly to the publisher doesn't mean they don't speak to each other.

A word to the wise, though. With many new magazines, financial concerns force the publisher, editor, circulation director, and advertising director to be crammed into the same body—yours. It's a burden, I can assure you, and you risk producing a substandard publication. Important tasks will go undone. If you should find yourself in this position, I highly recommend tightening the money belt in other areas and hiring an assistant. If your strengths are with numbers, hire someone with editorial know-how. Or vice versa. Do you get all in a tizzy when you visit a newsstand? Do you straighten up the rack, put everyone in their appointed places, and decide who has the choicest newsstand real estate? Do you love to receive direct mail pieces from magazines? Do you pour over every word, or do you chunk them in the trash without even opening them? Do you love to talk to people and try to sell them merchandise—be it Girl Scout cookies, vacuum cleaners, or advertisements? Assess your strengths and weaknesses as they relate to your magazine and hire the polar opposite as your assistant.

> **With many new magazines, financial concerns force the publisher, editor, circulation director, and advertising director to be crammed into the same body—yours.**

Editor

Pay special attention when selecting your editor. This position is not as it seems. Though the editor is charged with actually creating the magazine, she spends about 85% of the day managing people rather than words. If you like to write, this job may not be for you. Editors don't write—they don't have time to write. Instead, they juggle staff members, freelancers, photographers, and whoever else has been hired to generate content. The editor's major function is to *assemble* the creativity rather than to *produce* it.

Creatively, the editor is the captain of the ship who keeps one eye on the lighthouse at all times, who steers the crew toward the editorial concept. However, the editor must also have a modicum of math sense. The publisher will hand the ship's captain a budget, which she must spread out over the production process. The editor must decide the value of each word, the value of each writer, the value of each photograph, and so forth. Essentially, the publisher decides how much money the magazine will spend on content and the editor allocates the funds to the creative side of the flowchart.

> Essentially, the publisher decides how much money the magazine will spend on content and the editor allocates the funds to the creative side of the flowchart.

Managing Editor

When it comes to the nitty-gritty of magazine production, the managing editor takes charge. This person handles the day-to-day production duties like making sure freelancers actually receive their assignments and making sure the magazine receives its work. The managing editor pretty much runs the show after the editor hands over the content assignments.

Art Director

Reporting directly to the editor and working side-by-side with the managing editor is the art director. The art director is the creative staffer in charge of taking the words, the pictures, the creative juices, and blending them all together into an interesting and orderly publication. The art director actually builds the ship that the editor has been dreaming of navigating to the lighthouse. Thus, you need to find an incredibly talented, creative person to fill this spot. Any chimpanzee can drop copy on a blank page, but it takes a special eye to capture the reader with a clever, well-conceived design. Find that person.

CONCLUSION

Along with these positions outlined here, I recommend hiring an office manager or some form of glorified secretary to help out the publisher and editor. So, in terms of in-house staff, the only real requirements are the publisher, the editor, and this assistant. Everybody else—the art director, the writers, the ad sales staff, the photographers—can be freelancers. You can hire freelancers to handle circulation, advertising, even headline writing if you're that lazy.

But be warned. If you do not have a strong editor, you may wind up with a disjointed, confused publication. If your editor cannot properly synthesize the material and give it a solid, consistent voice, readers will know it's the work of freelancers and they'll lose interest.

Do not cave in to freelancers who attempt to set their words in stone. If they complain about minor editorial revisions made in the name of maintaining editorial voice, then look elsewhere for copy. The magazine's voice is sacred. It's the personality that endears the reader to your publication. The only time you relinquish your grasp of editorial voice is for the sake of your columnists. If Bill Clinton is writing a piece on life in the White House, it needs to sound like Clinton, not necessarily like *Rolling Stone* or *George*.

So, in the end, the publisher guides all. Beneath the publisher, you have the editor to guide the creative ship. The two must work together well, and rule the office, not with iron fists, but with creative spirit and solid financial know-how.

Are you up to it?

NOTES

....

....

....

....

....

....

....

....

....

....

....

....

....

....

....

....

....

....

David Lauren is president and editor-in-chief of Swing, *published by* Swing Magazine Corporation *in New York. The first issue of* Swing, *the magazine for those of the twenty-something Swing generation, was published in 1994.*

Interview:

David Lauren
Swing

Let's start with the idea for *Swing*.

I started the magazine when I was a student at Duke University, my sophomore year. I had an idea to do a magazine that I thought was needed on campus. We had the student newspaper, which was really about things going on in the school that were not really pertinent to our lives—things like how long the lines were in the cafeteria and how long a teacher should wait for tenure—and I found that to be very boring.

And I think a lot of young people, such as myself, had questions about what life would be like on the outside when you graduated, and how you could use your education. We wanted to talk to well-known people who were successful, and we wanted to talk to young people our age who were breaking ground in their respective industries.

At the time, there was a feeling that the market was very tight. We were in a recession and young people were scared that they wouldn't be able to get started. I was seeing all of these young entrepreneurs getting started, and I wanted to tell their stories to sort of inspire ourselves. There were also a lot of issues going around in politics— Clinton was being elected, the savings and loan scandal was happening, and no one really understood how it affected their lives, how it affected college, getting a job, starting a business, paying a mortgage, buying a car, getting married—the questions of people in their twenties.

So we set out to do a magazine that really reflected what we were interested in. I gathered some friends of mine together and we were able to hold meetings on campus. We financed it by getting a grant for about $4,000 from the president of Duke University. This money helped us do our first issue, and thereafter we got advertising from the community, from local stores.

How did you make the transition from being a Duke-only magazine to a national publication? Did it follow you when you graduated?

No. I did it for three years, and by the end of our senior year, some of my friends were going off to law school and medical school and all of that stuff, and I didn't know exactly what I wanted to do yet. I started to take the idea around to people whom I thought might be interested in helping me develop it. I brought it to friends of mine who were young writers or editors or photographers, and I wanted to see what they thought. Because we already had the magazine on newsstands, I got several calls from distributors and wholesalers who thought that the magazine was marketable.

Once we found a market and generated enough interest, I started to put together a business plan. Then I put a few people together whom I thought could help me develop the magazine at a more mature and professional level. We went out and spoke to different entrepreneurs and investment people and magazine experts to do some research, and then we just launched it. We were able to get it out about a year-and-a-half after I graduated.

What problems did you encounter?

Well, we're still encountering them. There were a million problems. We came into it with inexperience, but with the ability to try to start something from nothing. In essence, what you have is a blank slate. With every positive thing that happens, you fear what you are missing, what you are not doing right. We didn't have experience working at

twenty different magazines. In fact, I had almost no experience except for working for a couple of weeks at *Rolling
Stone*. Putting out a magazine was really just instinct for
what I thought people my age were interested in.

Everything was new—things like how you design a page,
how you make it consistent through the whole book, how
you edit a story, how you make the photography reflect
that, how you write cover lines, how you get an image that
is provocative, how you make it sell compared to other
magazines, how you go out and get ads. I mean, each of
these presented a problem and a frustration and required
a professionalism that we needed to develop.

I think people respected us for our instincts and for just
going for it.

**Let me pick out one of those things you said you had a prob-
lem with—recruiting advertising. How did you overcome that?**

We are still going through the frustrations of trying to get
ads. I think we went in very honestly. We said, "Listen, this
is a magazine that does not exist. There is a need for this
magazine."

We explained the size of the market—there are sixty-two
million people in their twenties. And we explained what
magazines were out there. We said most of the magazines
that target this age group are primarily music, fashion, and
celebrity gossip. A young person today, such as ourselves,
is looking at how the world is important and how he or
she can do better in it. What are the political issues that
need to be connected to us? Politics, sports, technology,
entertainment—all these things were really important to
young people, and they were not being addressed.

We began to see ourselves almost like a *Time* magazine or
a *Vanity Fair* for people in their twenties, but with the
issues and the personalities that connected to us.

**How important do you think it is for a new magazine to fill a
niche or a need?**

Well, the thing is that you never know how big that niche
is. I think that when we started, people said there is no

need for a magazine like this. They said young people don't read. And we said, yes, they do.

So, I think it's most important that you believe there is a market there, that you use your instincts, and that you are connected to your audience. There will always be someone with doubts, but I think we have proven there is a hole there that needs to be filled, and people who were not having their needs served elsewhere are buying this magazine.

When people told you there was no need for *Swing*, did you become discouraged?

Always. With every high, there's a low. No matter how big the market is, there is always someone who doesn't understand you. Being inexperienced, you not only have to prove yourself to the outside world, but you also have to prove it to the people you work with so they understand that you have a clear vision.

When you have experience, and you've been through it fifty times, people will assume that you know what you're doing. When you have to start from scratch, it's important that you be very strong in your sense of vision. A lot of times that comes with experience, so there's a double catch right there.

I think it has taken a lot of work to define myself, and I think that comes with my own maturation. I think that when you look at different pages in the magazine, you can see the growth. We definitely have always had frustrations trying to explain why a certain image reflected the story or why that story was even necessary.

With a magazine, you are always relying on the people around you. So you must make sure you can motivate the staff and you must make sure they understand your vision. That is very important.

What did you do, personally, to keep yourself going?

I had to remind myself that it's never that bad. We have had moments where ads were falling out, stories were coming in in terrible condition. You feel like you need to get outside, like your head is exploding. And that happens, probably once a month, when we are closing the magazine. It really does.

Inevitably, there is a low, and then you wake up for a couple of days, and you feel really depressed and frustrated, and you feel like you are not going to top yourself, and no one is going to like it, and they won't come back to the magazine.

I think the goal is to find distractions in your life, no matter what industry you are in. Whether you work out and do sports, find a boyfriend or a girlfriend—just get some perspective. I think it is very important to get some outside-people contact, because being at work can be a vacuum. You need always to understand that there is something bigger and more important than what you are doing. Sometimes, when I am working, it becomes everything, and once in a while when you step out and you realize that someone on the street is starving, you say, "You know what, life's not so bad." It gives you some perspective.

What did you look for when recruiting your staff?

I think the most important thing is to find people who are smart and who understand your vision, or who are willing to understand it—people who are respectful and self motivated.

I recruited people from various places. Generally, I would meet one person and he or she would introduce me to someone else. You have to network from there on out. We've run ads in papers, we've put signs up on the Internet for open jobs. But, generally, one person introduces you to another person and then you hire a managing editor, and he introduces you to a senior editor, and she introduces you to an ad director and it just grows like that somehow. But sometimes you just have to make some random calls. I might call other editors or even hire a head hunter if I have to.

What about flexibility? How important do you think it is to stick to your original concept?

Well, it's a combination. If you don't stick to your vision, then you're following someone else. And I think that's a problem. But if you have a vision, and your vision expands as you learn things, then that's fine.

There is a real problem in following other people, and, today, I think the tendency is for magazines to look like each other. People think that if one magazine is doing it, and it is successful, then that's the formula. Everybody runs a celebrity, and everybody seems to run certain colors and certain fonts and all of that. After a while it gets boring, and the person who was original stands out. And sometimes the timing is either too early or too late.

So you really have to bridge the gap. You want to understand your reader, and you have to observe and listen. But the best writer and the best editor really listen to the people around them and get a sense of what's going on.

You know, a magazine is a vehicle for the people who are interested in explaining their voices. But you have to be very clear about who you are when you're editing pieces. If you assume that everybody in the world loves a certain issue and feels a certain way, and if that's where you stand, then you might find yourself very lost.

Would you have done anything differently?

Yeah, I would, probably. I think it's great to start something without experience, to have that energy and to be dynamic and take a lot of gambles. But I also think that it probably would have been great to have known a little bit more. I think, probably, a lot of time and a lot of money gets wasted in developing ideas that could have been done in other ways, with more experience.

What I would change are simple things. But I think that, in order to learn it as fast, you have to start it yourself. I think that I've learned more about different sides of this business in a month, any given month, than I would have if I didn't have this position that I'm in.

What advice would you give someone who's launching a new magazine?

Make sure that you are ready to work hard, and make sure that you are confident about your idea. That's it.

NOTES

· ·

· ·

· ·

· ·

· ·

· ·

· ·

· ·

· ·

· ·

· ·

· ·

· ·

· ·

· ·

· ·

· ·

For the most part, accountants do not launch magazines. These much-maligned professionals are not necessarily known for their creativity. But you are. The catch is that you have to know something about money, too.

THE BUDGET 11

Conversely, the entrepreneur types who do dream, who do create concepts from passion and devotion, usually can't crunch a number to save their lives.

So where does that leave us? With a budget chapter you're probably none-too-excited about reading, and I'm none-too-excited about writing.

Building a sound budget is tough. It requires you, the over-romanticized idea machine, to quash your emotion and fiddle with a calculator. You may not have to know how to amortize depreciating capital investment, but you'll certainly have to hunker down and let reality smack you in the wallet.

REMEMBER, IT'S A BUSINESS

Repeat after me: A magazine is a business. Your concept and a buck fifty will buy you a cup of coffee. If it is stolen, you cannot sue for plagiarism. It's a magazine idea, not a patent or a copyright. And if nobody likes your concept, or if it is poorly executed, you cannot get your money back. Plain and simple. You and your investors are in it for the money, and it should be run with that motivation.

In order to execute your master plan with creative freedom and financial confidence, you must have the proper amount of venture capital. Cold, hard cash.

Therefore, as is true with any new business, being properly capitalized is crucial. If the concept is sound, then the execution of that concept becomes the next unavoidable step. In order to execute your master plan with creative freedom and financial confidence, you must have the proper amount of venture capital. Cold, hard cash.

But not your own. No magazine is a sure thing. If you want a wealthy investor to come knocking, you must draw the fly with honey. The more sound your budget, the more likely you are to earn the confidence of a venture capitalist.

Your budget can be broken into two parts: The prelaunch and the launch.

THE PRELAUNCH BUDGET

The prelaunch budget is a slippery beast. The number of variables it can contain are endless. It's wide open to cover the cost of whatever sound strategy or harebrained scheme you can conjure up in order to get your publication into the hands and thoughts of as many readers and advertising agencies as possible. In short, it is designed to pay for your prelaunch strategy.

As you probably know, there are a million ways to launch a magazine. You could print up a bunch of subscription cards and drop them from an airplane, purchase thirty minutes of air time for an infomercial, or claim to be Elvis' love child and hope the press notices. The two primary strategies for launching are the first issue test and the direct mail test.

First Issue Test

The first issue test involves putting together the actual premiere edition of the magazine. That means the stories are real, the photographs are real, and the ads are real (for real products, but they may not have been paid for). This magazine goes through all the channels of distribution a regular magazine would and will end up on the same newsstands it should be perched on this time next year.

The difference is, you have not quit your day job. You have no commitment to this magazine past this first issue. All you can do, once the book is compiled and distributed, is sit back and wait. Do people flock to it as you've predicted, or does it turn their stomachs and send them packing?

Know the Numbers

How do you decide whether you should continue with the magazine? If the numbers come back and you've sold between 40% and 45% on the newsstand, and you've received between ½% and 2% of the subscription cards, then you've got a green light. All systems are go, and you can move forward to the next stage. Anything less than that and you should either close up shop or seriously reevaluate your publication.

> **If the numbers come back and you've sold between 40% and 45% on the newsstand, and you've received between ½% and 2% of the subscription cards, then you've got a green light.**

Concerning costs, you will incur a great deal of expense with your first issue. First of all, you must pay your printer up front. He does not sit around and wait for newsstand sales revenue or subscription money to roll in. He is first on your list of expenses and he gets paid when his services are rendered.

And his services are not cheap. The average magazine (for these purposes, we'll say between 68 and 74 pages with a mixture of black and white and color photography) runs between 75¢ and $1.50 per magazine. That figure fluctuates according to paper quality, the number of full-color pages, and the dimensions of your publication. Therefore, if you plan a press run of 20,000 copies, budget between $15,000 and $25,000.

By the time you add in all of your other expenses (which will be discussed later in the chapter) you may be swamped with bills totaling $100,000.

Direct Mail Test

The direct mail test is no cheaper. It, too, may run up to $100,000 if done correctly. For this strategy, you will not put together an actual issue of the magazine. Though you may whip up a dummy prototype, you will not be paying for a press run.

However, you will be renting names from a list broker. After you've put together your envelope of sales pitches and subscription offers, you drop those suckers in the mail and wait for the returns.

Sounds easy enough, but printing up the direct mail pieces in your promotional packet is pricey. Also, you have postage to contend with. If each envelope costs you 40¢ in postage and you've got 50,000 addresses, you're looking at a bill for $20,000—just for stamps! Add to that your printing costs and name rentals, and you'll be up to $100,000 in no time.

If 4% of the direct mail subscription cards are returned, then you could be sitting on a gold mine.

As with the first-issue test, there is a point at which you know you should continue. If 4% of the direct mail subscription cards are returned, then you could be sitting on a gold mine. It sounds crazy—4%—but it's true. If 4% subscribe to *Ant Farm Monthly* based solely on a marketing brochure, then imagine what the rest of the population will think of it on the newsstand!

Prelaunch Budget Overview

Before deciding which method to budget into your business plan, you should make sure a few points sink into your brain (and into your investors' brains as well).

First of all, there is no return on this initial investment. If you find a venture capitalist to bankroll your prelaunch activity, he or she must understand that the purpose of prelaunch marketing is not to begin retiring your debt, but to test the market's waters. Sell it to them as such. Otherwise, you'll end up biting the hand that feeds you.

All the money during this period is spent on nonrevenue-generating expenses. The money is gone. What they've invested in, hopefully, is a green light from either ad agencies or from readers. It is a test. Do we proceed, or do we count our losses and quit? It's seed money. Thus, you should sell your investors on the worthiness of your idea and on your passion. Don't make big promises of profit and fame.

Also, when selecting your method, bear in mind that having an actual magazine is a plus. The operative word during this phase is "promotion," and having a selling tool like a finished product can only help. The ad agencies and media outlets know it is a creative work. They know there are no formulas for cranking out a successful publication. Much of what will make your magazine successful will be the level of emotion it evokes from the opinion leaders. Though there are some good direct mail pieces out there, none pack the emotional wallop of a full-blown magazine.

THE LAUNCH BUDGET

Expenses

Once you've taken care of all your prelaunch expenses, you're ready for the big bucks. The initial $100,000 has been raised and spent like so much water. The market gives you the green light, and you're ready to roll. What do you do now?

Start raising more money. A lot more money. If you thought the prelaunch expenses racked up, wait until you see your first twelve months' operating expenses.

Prepress

For instance, approximately 33% of total cost is eaten up by manufacturing. More than just printing, this number includes such prepress technicalities as color separations and transference of the magazine from computer-generated binary code to press-ready plates. You don't need to know the specifics of what this stage involves right now, besides the fact that it can eat anywhere from $4,000 to $50,000 per issue, depending on the complexity and color intensity of your design.

Printing

And printing, as mentioned earlier, is pricey. If you put out 50,000 copies of a moderately colored 100-page magazine 6 times per year, you're looking at annual printing costs in the neighborhood of $375,000. If you're trying to pull off launching monthly, the bill shoots up to $750,000 during the first year of operation. Ouch.

If you put out 50,000 copies of a moderately colored 100-page magazine 6 times per year, you're looking at annual printing costs in the neighborhood of $375,000.

Salaries

Next, budget for your salaries. As you read in **The Staff** chapter, plan on hiring three people at an average salary of $22,500 (if you're in New York City, jack that up another five to ten grand). You may pay your art director more and your secretary less, but use $22,500 as a middle ground. Before you set that number in stone, you must pay unto Caesar what is Caesar's. As the employer, you have to tack on an additional 15% for Social Security and taxes. The new four-person total comes to $103,500.

Commission

That brings us to commission. This is another big expense most newcomers don't foresee. The three major commission outlays will be for advertising sales (20%), newsstand sales (60%), and subscription fulfillment (20%). If you sell 20 ad pages at $3,000 per page, you'll have to shell out $12,000 to your sales representative or to your rep agency.

If you print 50,000 copies, sell them at $4.95 each, and achieve a 40% sell-through, you'll be cutting a check to your distributor for approximately $60,000 and keeping about $40,000 for yourself.

As you read in **Circulation**, the distributor and wholesaler take a substantial chunk of your newsstand profits. If you print 50,000 copies, sell them at $4.95 each, and achieve a 40% sell-through, you'll be cutting a check to your distributor for approximately $60,000 and keeping about $40,000 for yourself. Pretty shabby, but that's the breaks.

Office Expenses

It may seem like you've been bled to death already, but you haven't scratched the surface of office expenses. You've got to pay the rent and utilities; buy furniture, computers, and software; pick out stationery, a fax machine, and laser paper; buy paper clips, coffee pots, wall hangings, magazine subscriptions, light bulbs, notepads, and flowers on National Secretary's Day. It adds up.

Then, you've got to get on the phone to your insurance agent and pick up some liability and health insurance just in case somebody gets hurt during the production of your magazine. No kidding.

Also, figure in your repayment of the investor's money—with interest. This number is entirely flexible and will most likely be determined by the accountant who gets between you and your venture capitalist.

Content Generation

And please, please, do not forget to include freelancers in your budget. Actually generating the content will cost you a pretty penny. Unless you plan to write and shoot everything yourself, you've got to budget fees for writers and photographers. Like all else, what you pay these folks fluctuates. Many magazines pay 10¢ per word for all copy, but the larger publications can afford to pay $3,000 and up for features. Photography is done the same way. You'll just have to work it out with the specific photographer concerning pay. Some may work for free just for the opportunity to be in a nationally distributed magazine, while others may send you to an early grave. Play it by ear.

The Launch Budget: Revenue

And now for the good news. Despite the nightmare of expenses, your magazine can make money. Otherwise, the hundreds of people who launch magazines every year would stick to their day jobs. Not only is it a fun way to let your imagination run wild and spill into the American psyche, but you can also use it to put food on the table and a fancy new car in the garage.

Circulation

The two primary sources of income for any magazine are circulation and advertising. Sure, single-copy sales are not the gold mine we all wish they could be, but you've also got subscription revenue steadily pouring in. Also, with single-copy sales, it may take up to six months to receive the money from your distributor. With subscriptions, the money is all up front and in the bank before you go to press. In that sense, this is the only business where lay-a-way is backwards. The customer pays, and the business doles out the product in set increments over a set period of time.

Advertising

With advertising revenue, you'll be turning a substantial profit. Minus the 20% for sales commission, advertising is the best way to get money in the bank. Assuming you outsource the sales staff, you can sit back, put out the magazine, and let the ad dollars roll in. You don't have to lure in the account executives with saucy cover lines or vivid colors as you do with the readers. Just keep circulation at a respectable level, and the salesmen will do the rest. Remember, you're doing a favor for these advertisers. They want to reach a particular kind of person, and you're delivering him or her on a silver platter. Stay focused on who that targeted reader is, and the advertisers will continue to send you money.

Stay focused on who that targeted reader is, and the advertisers will continue to send you money.

Venture Capital

Also, toss your investor's contributions into the revenue pot. You don't earn it the same way as other revenue, but you spend it all the same. Spread it out over a fiscal period and treat it like income.

Marketing

Finally, you've got the nebulous "miscellaneous" revenue generators. This takes into account such fundraisers as marketing tie-ins (coffee mugs, T-shirts, bumper stickers) and name rentals. Yes, just as you rented names for your direct mail campaign, other businesses may approach you for the same purpose. If your magazine is niched really well, your database of subscribers will eventually be valuable to somebody. So rent it out for cash. At 10¢ per name and a subscriber base of, say, 30,000, you can turn a $3,000 profit for simply existing. Never turn your nose up at profit. Be it $3,000 or $300,000, it all comes in handy when you're doing payroll.

CONCLUSION

As I've told a thousand magazine launchers before you, the numbers in this budget are worthless. Magazine publishing involves too many variables to allow you to pin money down to the bottom line. However, taking all of my suggestions into account in your budget will give you a solid piece of information to take to your investor.

Your patron wants to know your projections are as close to reality as possible. And then maybe even a little closer. So do that. Research specific costs in your area, from printing to staff salaries to computer software. Take an educated stab at what you cannot set in stone.

Once you've done this for your first year of operation, balancing revenue against expenses, project where you will be in four years. This is how long the average new magazine takes to reach maturity and turn the corner into net profit. Can you beat the clock and make money in year three? Your investor wants to know. Does every combination of variables ensure bankruptcy after six months? If that's the case, fess up.

After you've determined, to the best of your ability, what you will need to get by during the first year, double it. Ask the investor to cut you a check for twice what you think you'll need. Paper costs may go up, sales may go through the roof, or you may need another two or three staff members. Remember, the fastest way to go belly up is to be undercapitalized.

Remember, the fastest way to go belly up is to be undercapitalized.

And, if you forget everything else, just remember to have a beautiful relationship with your banker, your accountant, and your attorney. They are your friends. They are there to help you. Don't make them hate you because they can make your life (and your business plan) miserable. They can also make you rich.

Remember, it's a business.

NOTES

....

....

....

....

....

....

....

....

....

....

....

....

....

....

....

....

....

....

*Mike and Claire Stanley are the founders of **Longbows & Recurves**, the magazine of traditional bow hunting at its best. Published by Stanley Publications Inc., in Corinth, Mississippi, the magazine saw its first issue in winter 1996.*

Interview:
Mike & Claire Stanley
Longbows & Recurves

What attracted you to the magazine business?

It sounded like fun. I like to mess with my Macintosh. I liked business. I've been in advertising before, and I've been in accounting. I like to hunt. I like the topic.

I didn't have a clue about the magazine publishing business, but I just figured I could learn it. Of course, I did not know a whole lot about archery, but I have hunted all my life. I just hadn't bow hunted. I just started doing it.

The magazine business had some sort of appeal to me, though. It was creating something. It would be something that would be my own. It would be something we would sink or swim with together—my wife and I. I could not blame it on anybody else. I either worked hard and made it work, or did not work hard and it failed. Nobody to blame but me. I've always been sort of an entrepreneur with a real entrepreneurial spirit. I've wanted to do something on my own.

How did you raise the money?

I sold some land. I put my own money into it. That was mainly to buy a computer, I guess. Once I had that, I did a lot of research. I bought a faster computer.

While I was writing the business plan, I realized how much money I was going to need to make this work, to get over the hump. I realized the greatest amount of money that I would need would be about two-and-a-half years down the road, and I knew what the figure was. So that was my goal—just to figure out a way to accomplish that goal of raising "x" amount of money.

I've done a number of different things. I've had a private stock sale, and that has worked so far.

I looked at buying other magazines. I wrote the business plan, did my research, negotiated, and was about to do it when the deal changed. The owner decided he wanted more for the business than I was going to pay.

So I sat down and talked about it with my wife, and we picked a topic and decided we knew enough to start one ourselves.

I think I can do a whole lot better myself rather than taking one that is already out there and trying to improve on it. I think that is a good idea in some businesses—trying to make lemonade out of lemons—but in the magazine business, I now believe it's a little bit different. The creativity is a whole lot greater in this industry.

Is the ability to change essential in this business?

Yes, you have to be very flexible. I am having to learn how to do a lot of different things and not get all bent out of shape when things don't happen just right. It is not always going to go the same way.

What else have you learned?

Persistence. And I'm learning how to delegate things. I can't do it all by myself. I am not physically able to do everything, but we've got an office in the small business incubation system, which is a facility sponsored by the Small Business Administration. We don't know all the answers but there are people there who can help.

We've got an office along with ten other businesses that are starting up. We have access to a secretary who can type for us and work on the computer for us, we have access to a copier and a fax machine, and all that is included in the rent, so we can keep our overhead cost low. I have found some good friends in town, one who happens to be a professional editor and the other is a very good graphic designer. And they are growing with us.

How have you changed?

For my wife and me to get something done and stay married, I had to loosen up a considerable amount. It is a lot of pressure if you let it build up.

What benefits have you received?

The benefits have been very satisfying so far. We certainly have a long way to go, and we are not there by a long shot, but the work has been a kind of a high-five experience. I am not going to see any monetary rewards for a while. My projections show that if we stick with it, and if we execute our plans, then we can do that eventually. But it won't be within the next couple of years.

NOTES

....

....

....

....

....

....

....

....

....

....

....

....

....

....

....

....

....

Your next task in this monster of a business plan looks easy enough on the outside, but don't be fooled. It's a tough one. Your executive summary and contingency plan must explain your strategy for making a killing on the newsstand.

CONTINGENCY PLAN 12

Think about it: What tycoon with enough money to bankroll a magazine has the time to leisurely thumb through a forty-page business plan? None that I know (not that I know any). In fact, go ahead and assume the tycoon you unearth has no free time. Let that lighthouse guide your copy. In other words, you need to produce a clear, concise, and compelling summary of your entire business plan in no more than a single page. Besides a nice haircut and a new suit, this will be the first impression old moneybags has of you and your business acumen. So do it right.

Give this executive summary the same treatment you give your concept. Remember, the concept will remain constant for the life of the magazine. It is the guiding force, the original lighthouse that guides every move. The executive summary, then, is like a punching bag for the myriad business plan revisions you make along the way. You will kick, punch, and generally mistreat this poor document every time your numbers change, but its core elements will remain the same.

BASIC QUESTIONS

Each summary must answer four basic questions: What is the magazine going to be about, who will read it, where will the money come from, and how much do you need?

The first question will be addressed by a boiled down synthesis of your letter from the editor, your concept, and your table of contents. Use strong verbs, bright language, and convincing arguments. And keep it brief.

Identifying your reader may be difficult in such a tight setting. To be convincing, you'll need to beef it up with some basic statistics. Again, make sure you don't ramble on. You don't want to put your potential investors to sleep.

For the source of the revenue, you need to give a breakdown of the advertising, circulation, and competition analyses. Let them know your baby can make money on its own—a lot of money.

Finally, and most delicately, tell them what the damage is. How much are you asking for? Cut to the chase; give them a hard figure. Don't be cutesy and say your magazine is on sale for $499,999.95. Take their money seriously and be honest. They know how these things work and big numbers shouldn't scare them.

KNOW THYSELF

This executive sales pitch should be placed ahead of all else in your business plan. It's the nugget of data potential investors want to know first, and sometimes they may even want to hear you summarize your written plan. So, memorize it. Know it like you know your concept. Upside down, backwards, whatever. If you ask the editor-in-chief of *GQ* what the concept of his magazine is, what are the odds he'll say something like, "It's, uh, thick, and it, hmmm, makes money, and there's, like, Italian suits and stuff." Not likely. He'll probably rattle off the concept as it's printed in *SRDS*: "*GQ* addresses the people, places, ideas, and issues that shape men's personal expression, development, and experiences."

> **You are not selling potential investors your magazine— you're selling them a business plan.**

You need to coax this document into your potential investors' psyche in five minutes. After that, their eyes may glaze over and you've lost their attention for good. Remember, you are not selling them your magazine—you're selling them a business plan. It's less flashy, less interesting, and decidedly more expensive. That is why you need to be so well-prepared with your information. And that is why this first page to page-and-a-half is so important.

RISK ANALYSIS

Let's say they've read your executive summary and are still allowing you to take up their time. Perhaps they've begun flipping through the rest of the business plan. The next item on the list of things they want to see is called the contingency plan or risk analysis.

What is a risk analysis? Well, first define the word *entrepreneur*. An entrepreneur is someone who takes a calculated risk. A fool takes risks. What are the odds of jumping off the World Trade Center and not dying? A fool might take that risk. An entrepreneur would want to know the odds of surviving a jump from the WTC with a hidden parachute in your backpack. You may die anyway, but the rewards of possibly surviving and being famous are worth the risk.

Your business is like that leap. Your investors want to know how big the parachute is and how much it costs, how far the fall is, will you break a fingernail, your leg, or your neck, has anyone done this before you, and how big will their share of the windfall be? These questions are answered in the risk analysis.

CATEGORY RESEARCH

Research the survival rate of magazines in your category. What have their survival rates been? With restaurants, only one in ten survive the first year of business. For a magazine, half die the first year, and after four years, three out of ten are still alive. In the 1980s, only two out of ten survived. Your investors will want to know this. Be honest. Tell them that things are looking good for the industry, but it will take four years to reach maturity and turn the corner into profits.

This being the case, research your category for the last five years and determine the survival rate. Overall, three out of ten survive, but in the men's category, 210 have been launched while only ten are still on newsstands.

That's a survival rate of about 5%. Is this a good thing to tell your investors? If you're in this predicament, you better come up with a convincing argument as to why you want to launch in that category.

PLAN AHEAD

Also as part of your risk analysis, your investor will want to know that you've planned ahead. He or she will want to know that you've imagined every possible scenario for what could befall the investment. For instance, I have recently been working on the launches of two magazines, *Alive* and *@Austin*. *Alive* is an Egyptian magazine which, as announced by its publisher in an interview in the *Utne Reader*, was to be launched in the spring of 1997. *@Austin* was to be launched in November 1996. Well, things happen, and *Alive* had a fall 1997 launch and *@Austin* was pushed to late spring of that same year.

What does this do to your business plan? The contingency plan will outline that if funding is made available by June, then the launch will be in April. If there is a delay, it will have to be pushed another six months to a year. The reason we pushed *@Austin* from November to April is because launching in January or February is suicide. People are recuperating financially from the holidays and don't want to shell out for a new magazine. Same thing applies for a June or July launch. Avoid these months because most people are out of town, mail piles up, credit card bills from the trip to Disneyland come in—you get the point. On the other hand, April is income tax refund season.

PREDICT SCENARIOS

This is the role a contingency plan serves. You outline solutions before the problems present themselves. What if you publish your first issue, the media loves it, you love it, but newsstand sales come back and you realize you only sold twelve copies? What do you do? Reduce printing from 20,000 to 10,000? Use brighter colors on the cover? Sell it door to door? The contingency plan addresses this. What if you put the issue on the newsstand and, kaboom!, you sell out? Do you double your press run? Do you go from printing six issues a year to twelve? Sometime success can be as big a burden as failure. Well, maybe not quite as big.

Consider as many potentially hazardous variables as possible and provide a clear strategy for each scenario.

PLAY IT COOL

The contingency plan should remind your investor that there are a million variables in this business, and that you will not scrap your plans on an issue-to-issue basis. The key is to play it cool. If one issue doesn't do well on the newsstand, you needn't do a 180-degree back flip somersault to fix it. Give things time either to correct themselves or to become a clear and present danger. Consider as many potentially hazardous variables as possible and provide a clear strategy for each scenario.

The question most likely to be shouted in your ear is, "When do I get my money back?" Do not be afraid of this question. Plan for it. Have a prepared answer or you won't get a dime. Most importantly, give a stern warning that your magazine is a slow investment. It isn't Netscape stock. It will take several years to turn a profit. Then, in the fine print of the contract, or spoken at lightning speed like the guy in the old Fed Ex commercials, inform them that previous performance is not an indicator of future performance and they may lose all or part of the money they sink in the project. Seriously, there is a big fat chance nobody will buy the magazine and they'll be out twenty grand or a hundred grand or even a million bucks.

OTHER PEOPLE'S MONEY

I warn everybody I consult with not to start a magazine with their own money. Do not mortgage your house, your boat, or your farm. Find somebody else who can absorb the losses in stride. And don't quit your day job prematurely.

If you are smart enough and creative enough to produce a business plan for a new magazine, you should be able to transfer a little more creative energy into convincing investors to give you money. The executive summary and contingency plan should be the crux of this sales pitch.

Give it thought and keep it brief.

The first issue of Mode, *the fashion and lifestyle magazine edited for full-figured women, was published in spring 1997. Cofounded by Nancy Nadler LeWinter and Julie Lewit, the magazine is published by Lewit & LeWinter Inc./Pantheon International Ltd. in New York.*

Interview:

Julie Lewit
Mode

What magazines have you launched?

The first one I launched was *Savvy*, and I was associate publisher of that. Then there was *New York Woman*, where I was the founding publisher. Then there was *Mirabella*, where, again, I was founding publisher. And now *Mode*. But with *Mode*, I have two partners with whom I own it. So it is very different for us.

Talk about the launch process of each of these.

It goes so far back. Well, even though I was part of the launch of *Savvy*, I was not a part of the idea process. I was more involved in the advertising of it. But with *New York Woman* and *Mode*, I was there from the very beginning.

With *Mode*, my partner Nancy and I are not only involved in the marketing of it and the positioning of it, but also we are heading up the editorial process.

The idea for *Mode* literally came from when Nancy and I were having breakfast one morning and we were looking at an article about the fact that America is expanding, and that the average size in this country is a size 14. We were talking about what we wanted to do with our business and partnership, and we sort of looked at each other and said, "That's it." There is no fashion magazine for women who are not size 4, 6, 8, or 10. And what we wanted to do is create a fashion magazine for women who are not the perfect size 6, but the perfect size 16. So that was the very beginning.

So that afternoon we asked our assistant to dig through Lexis-Nexis {a computerized, research database} and take down every piece of information there was about women that were not size 6. We wanted anything over size 14 or anything that talked about weight in America—the perception of women, full-figured women, fat women, just whatever.

What came back was a very informational database that was just floating around. There wasn't a huge amount of stuff, but there were some stories about discrimination against women who were overweight. I'm so reluctant to even use these words at this point because they are so incorrect—about being overweight, the fattening of America.

We found that women who aren't your standard stilt-like figures were discriminated against, they could not find any clothes, they were second-class citizens, and they were not being treated properly. This was like the last real prejudice in the world, and we felt that we should keep looking at all of this.

We looked through every possible publication we could find, and there was not a lot. There was *BBW*, which stands for "Big, Beautiful Woman." We talked to some of our friends in the business who were bigger than size 14, and we asked them about their perception of fashion.

We did not do our own focus groups, but friends of ours were serving as a sort of a focus group in regard to developing a line of clothing for fuller-figured women. And what became very clear was that there was this tremendous void. This is not an unemotional business. Women who were size 18, 20, 22, 24, or whatever, felt left out, angry, and they were not pleased as consumers or as magazine readers.

And then we also looked at what was happening in the fashion and retail worlds. In speaking to retailers, we found that for the stores that carried some selection, the larger sizes were a very, very good part of their business. They had fewer markdowns, and the return investment per square footage was far greater than it was in what is called the misses sizes.

So the retailers really looked at this as a growth opportunity, but they still were not very comfortable with it. They recognized that this was a big part of their business but they were not quite ready to expand in a sense and some were. For example, Saks has just celebrated its first year doing it, so they are very much in the forefront. Bloomingdale's is very successful with its great looking department for women who are full figured. Even Sears, for example, has started to take a very serious look at this. I think 17% or 18% of its total business is in women's sizes, so we are talking about a huge amount of business. That says there is a readiness on the part of the retailers to go for it.

We also found that the number of manufacturers and designers for larger women has increased. In fact, it has multiplied many fold in the last seven years. Seven years ago, there were 200 vendors and manufacturers who were creating fashions for full-figured women, and now there are about 2,000.

There were all of these pieces like a puzzle that became very clear all of a sudden, almost like a mosaic. It was just right there in front of us. There was a real need here, so we started to speak to some people in the magazine world, some editorial people that Nancy and I worked with in our past careers. A couple of people were full-figured themselves and were in the fashion industry, and they confirmed the same thing. There were models that were available, and there were photographers who would want to work with women who were full-figured, and so, again, everything indicated that the timing was so right.

At the same time there was a huge backlash against the Kate Moss syndrome. I think it was about a year-and-a-half ago when Calvin Klein pulled some controversial ads, and there was a huge amount of fury. Someone actually pulled their advertising out of *British Vogue* because they felt the models were just too anorexic and that they were supporting a really bad body image for women.

All of these things became a real topic of interest, and it's like I always say, great ideas do not happen in a vacuum. I really believed that it was in the air. It was just one of those moments when it all started to percolate, and I can honestly say that Nancy and I were in the right frame of mind at the right moment at the right place. And since our background is fashion publishing, we could take a look at it from the magazine consumer's angle.

Initially, we started to talk to some marketers whose opinions we trusted, and every time they said it was a great idea. The question was always, "How well can you execute it?" That was their greatest reservation, because magazines for full-figured women were usually very second rate, really chintzy, as if they were put together somewhere in the basement. There was no real photography. They just did not look right.

So our goal focused on providing a professional looking fashion magazine. A woman who may feel like a second-class citizen would not feel that way when she picked up this magazine. We were absolutely certain that what we wanted to do was to create a product that looked like any other fashion magazine. It would be printed on the same paper, it would have the best photographers, it would have the best models, it would have the best possible clothes, and a woman would be proud to carry it around.

Is it necessary for a magazine concept to be "needed"?

It's very important. But there are a couple of things that you really have to look for. The idea has to be unique. It cannot be a mutual idea. The second thing is you have to be able to describe your idea in one sentence. You cannot have a magazine idea that, when you explain it to somebody, they look at you like, "Huh?"

The idea should be clear-cut and the need has to be there, or at least the perceived need has to be there. And we felt very strongly that the need was there.

What came next?

We had the idea, and we felt that we really wanted to create a terrific magazine, so we talked to our financial partner, Stanley, who has a magazine company. He does not launch anything of *Mode*'s scale, but he has a great deal of experience in circulation and manufacturing.

So he thought it was a great idea. Even though he has never done a fashion magazine, he recognized that this has legs. He is in charge of the distribution, the circulation, and the manufacturing. So we were assured from the very beginning that the magazine would be out there and that it would be printed in the best possible way.

In the meantime, Stanley, Nancy, and I probably spent six weeks coming up with a title of the magazine. I cannot tell you how many hundreds of names we had.

How did you narrow it down?

We really wanted to keep it short. It is always better to keep it under seven letters. Launching *Mirabella*, we could hardly fit it on the masthead. Nancy was the launch director for the American launch of *Marie Claire*, and that has a few letters in it, too. So we really wanted to keep it short. Also, you have to look at what letters look good. It really comes down to graphics.

What did you look for in staff?

We wanted people who were were very experienced and whose work we just loved. The criteria was that the people had to love the idea. They got excited about it and wanted to really make a difference in these women's lives. So, with a great staff, we could create a magazine that was the best and would really surprise the reader.

The whole process began. Our first shoot was the first time a full-figured woman was shot in the way of a real fashion shoot. Very deductional, very trendy, not at all catalogue-like. We used a very, very good photographer who used a new technique in photography.

Model Kate Dillon is a size 16. She was shot in a very cool

way. We stocked her very coolly, got really designer stuff, totally noncatalogue looking. It just came back looking phenomenal.

That was the first thing that we did. That showed us, yes indeed, you can really shoot women who are not your perfect size 6 in a way that looks fabulous. It gave us a great deal of encouragement to proceed.

At the same time, we started to talk to the marketing community, the advertisers, the retailers. Since then, we've been working sixteen hours a day, nonstop.

What about advertisers?

They loved it.

They recognized a need?

I think some advertisers like to be first, and some generally do not like to be first. There are some in-between who will go with an idea or who will take a wait-and-see attitude. In our case, even the ones in the middle tended to say, "Hey, this is really a good idea." I think the major concern they had, which has since been eliminated, was what it would look like. We have every major advertiser, every major retailer, and every major cosmetics company. That is the big difference in execution.

Also, Nancy's and my level of expertise won them over. She launched *Marie Claire*; she was the publisher of *Esquire*, advertising director of *Vogue*, business manager for *Glamour*, and a lawyer prior to that. I was the publisher of *Mademoiselle*, launched *Mirabella*, launched *New York Woman*, was the vice-president of marketing at *Esquire*, launched *Savvy*, worked at *Woman's Day* and *Ms.*

So we have a lot of magazine experience. Thus, the marketers feel pretty comfortable that if Nancy and Julie are involved in this, it is not going to look schlocky.

How do you maintain that quality?

Our second issue was probably 50% better than our first. I have become much braver, and we are pushing the envelope much more. There is a certain tentativeness when you do something for the first time. You are not quite surefooted.

I think we did a very good first issue—the reception has been phenomenal. But we will always refer to it as a very good first issue, not a great issue. There is a qualifier on "first." We don't feel that we can rest on our laurels.

What does bravery have to do with it?

Surefootedness is key—getting the response from the readers, from community. I have never launched a magazine that had the kind of outpouring or response that *Mode* had. It was unbelievable. We have gotten 500 letters in the first month. We've bound the letters. As we are getting them in, we make a photocopy of it and bind it.

It is overwhelming. What almost 99.9% of the women have said is, "Thank you, thank you, thank you. It's about time. You validated, you confirmed, you made me feel pretty." Women are using words like, "This has been an epiphany."

A reader can finally look at the model and say, "I can look that way. I can wear that. I don't have to be relegated to polyester tent hoods."

There are 16 million women out there who have to think about it constantly. "I want this, but I cannot have it." Here is the land of the free and free choice, but when you walk into a store, they look at you like you're a freak of nature at size 16.

These women are saying to us for the first time, "We feel there is somebody out there who knows how we live." I mean, that is overwhelming.

We have now been covered by every major television station. We have been invited to come back to the *Today* show for the third time. Never has that happened to either Nancy or me. Newspapers all over the country have articles about *Mode*. One newspaper described us as standing out from the other fashion magazines like a sunflower in a field of string beans. We have been in *USA Today* and

U.S. News and World Report. I mean, the coverage has been completely unbelievable. So that means to us that, not only are the readers there, but this make news. So there is something to it.

What are the main problems you encountered along the way from conception to printing?

I think we were amazingly fortunate. We did not have huge problems. Generally, though, the biggest problem is money. Great idea, but if you don't have backers, and if you don't have your own money, it is really difficult to get it out there.

The second thing is actually doing it. I hear so many ideas from so many people out there. They're walking around with really good ideas. They just cannot figure out how to get them done.

How did you overcome that?

We're doers. We know how to do it. That is something I cannot explain to you. Ideas are a dime a dozen, but doing it is a whole different thing.

It's having discipline, having the conviction, and having the resolve, and not just sitting around thinking about it. There are very few people who do that.

I am sure there are tons of magazine ideas floating around journalism schools, where students spend hours talking about it in classes. I know, because I lecture in journalism. There are tons and tons of ideas, but very few people will actually go out and do it.

Does flexibility play a role for you?

You need a tremendous amount of flexibility because you never know what will happen. You have to be really, really attuned to what the market wants and to what the readers want. You cannot lock yourself in to ideas.

I will never forget—I once had this conversation with somebody who was launching a magazine for the first time. The person is going to remain nameless, but he was considered a magazine guru by many, and he was going to launch his first magazine with a huge amount of backing from a very major company. And he came to me because I had launched many magazines at this point, and he asked for my advice.

It was very clear from the beginning that the last thing he wanted to hear was my advice because he was absolutely dead-set on how he was going to present his magazine to the world.

I said, "You can't do that because the worst thing you can do is pin yourself into a corner. You don't know who is going to respond to your magazine yet. You do not know how it is going to change from the period you get the idea until it gets on paper. Even after that, you make so many changes."

You have to be so flexible. Something that looks like a great idea today, tomorrow will look like, "How did I think of that! This is really lousy, that is dumb!"

I loved this cover for the second issue, and two days later, I said, "How could I have loved this? It's terrible." Originally, I thought it was fabulous. My partner did not, and we were fighting over it. I remember thinking it was fantastic, and she said, "No, I don't think so."

People agreed with me. They thought it was fantastic. I assure you, what I thought was fantastic, and what I now think is fantastic, would make you look at me like I have three heads.

You have to be incredibly flexible. This is where perfectionism does not work. A perfectionist is always right, but I can always change my mind. Always. And if you have a better idea, I will listen to you, and I am very willing to say it's good.

So maybe I'm not right all the time. There is no such thing as being right or wrong—it is simply having different thoughts. So I do not think one can be a perfectionist in this business, because that shows inflexibility.

How did your life in magazines begin?

I was on the other side actually. I was on the agency side. The last job I had at the advertising agency was associate media director, and *Ms* magazine came and made a presentation. The next day, the magazine called and asked if I wanted to switch and come over and sell for them.

I was getting really bored with the agency business. So I thought, "Hey, why not?" I spent the first six months of my career as a salesperson crying. Very unfeminist behavior, I must add.

I had been this media princess at the time who was taken out to lunch and wined and dined, and if I called somebody, he returned my phone call. And the next day, I was a nobody. I was this salesperson from *Ms* magazine whom nobody called back.

That was my first sales job. And I went from *Ms* to *Woman's Day*, and then I launched *Savvy*. That was my first executive job.

Ever had problems raising money for a launch?

I tried to launch my own magazine between *Mademoiselle* and starting my own business with Nancy. I tried to launch a magazine called *About Face*, which was a beauty magazine. We tried to raise money for that, but we just couldn't do it. Good idea, but we could never raise the money. Never made it.

How do you advise prospective magazine launchers?

The idea has to be very sound, very solid. It has to have a new angle. It has to have a constituency that the marketing community will feel is big enough. You cannot publish a magazine for four people.

You have to be able to execute on some scale. It has to have the potential to be a bigger magazine. It cannot be a small idea. It has to have enough people. If you take a look at fashion magazines—and this was another reason why we felt so strongly about *Mode*—the actual number of women who buy fashion magazines is three million. But there are roughly a hundred million women in this country who are eighteen and over. What does that tell you? It means that ninety seven million women do not buy a fashion magazine.

So ask the question, "Why don't they buy it?" Look at that market. Chances are that sixty million of that ninety seven million are not buying it because there's nothing in it for them. Most likely because there's a size discrepancy. So we have a potential audience of sixty million women who never buy a fashion magazine. Now that's a market. If only 1% of sixty million women buy this magazine, we have a magazine that has six hundred thousand circulation.

That is more than enough to start off with. That is something that is a worthwhile. Only 1%.

Now, we've put out the magazine. Just on our blow-in cards, we are getting 8%. At that, we have the potential of having roughly four and a half million circulation. Which could mean that *Mode* has the potential to become the single largest fashion magazine in this country.

So that's my advice. That's what you have to determine. What is the potential? Are you willing to do a magazine for left-handed doctors? Chances are, you will have a very small magazine. It could be a great idea, but how many people are going to respond to it. And if it is a great idea, you had better charge six hundred dollars for a subscription. Because maybe the five hundred left-handed doctors who would be interested in this idea will all subscribe to it. One hundred percent of the universe is miraculous. And the magazine could be the absolute cat's meow for all five hundred doctors. Of course, you'd have a circulation of five hundred.

Do you think everyone should take a chance?

Well, having taken so many chances, I always feel that you should take a chance. But I feel your chance should be moderated by reason.

You should not fall in love with your idea. If you fall in love with your idea, any kind of perspective, any kind or reasonable thinking, is going to go out the window. It is just like when you fall in love with somebody, you never notice the warts on his nose. Everything is gorgeous until one morning you wake up and say, "Oh my God, look at the wart on his nose! How did I never notice that?"

So you cannot fall in love with the idea because you lose all perspective. You wouldn't be reasonably sound in your judgment.

Be flexible and be willing to bend. Something might not have been the great idea you thought it was. If you have all the money in the world, go for it.

However you want to spend your money, whether you want to go to Tiffany's or you want to launch a magazine, it is your money. Do what you feel good about. If you have the luxury of doing whatever you want to do, you might as well launch a magazine. It's great fun.

Now that you've got your business plan in tip-top shape, it's time to give it life. It's time for the prototype. No business plan is complete without a mock-up, or dry run, of the real magazine. So let's do it.

THE PROTOTYPE 13

In the perfect universe, a prototype is a true representation of the physical aspects of your magazine. The point is to provide a taste of the appearance and nature of the publication. As authentically as possible, create a prototype of the same dimensions, paper stock, color scheme, and design the original you will have in the coming months.

No matter how crazy you make it, this dry run should sum up the average of what the real magazine will be like. For instance, many prototypes will insert blank pages just to match the weight and thickness of the future issues. Also, some ambitious magazine launchers will print two or three different covers and include them in the first several pages of the prototype. Of course, you'd never do this in the real magazine, but for the prototype, it shows you know exactly where you're headed. Not only does it illustrate the strength of your logo in more than one design, but it also sets the overall tone of the cover design and shows a well-rehearsed creative spirit.

BUT WHY?

The prototype has three main purposes. First, it makes your media kit complete. Media buyers at ad agencies will want to know exactly what they're getting into, so the better the prototype, the better your chances at swaying an opinion.

Second, the prototype is a great resource for focus groups. When you gather four or five folks around a table, feedback will be more accurate if participants are critiquing an actual magazine rather than a typed-out mission statement and table of contents. They can really help you focus on the many elements that go into it. If you're publishing *Commuter Monthly*, you might not have thought to print on a light paper stock that can be easily rolled up and shoved in a coat pocket. Your focus group will tell you this.

Your prototype is an excellent testing ground for you and your staff. It can set the boundaries for what you can and cannot achieve.

Finally, your prototype is an excellent testing ground for you and your staff. It can set the boundaries for what you can and cannot achieve. If you have dreams of publishing a 200-page magazine with 20 departments, 8 features, and 250 photographs, you may be in for a rude awakening. And I promise you, it's better to find this out while putting together your prototype rather than your first real issue.

THE DESIGN

Besides illustrating your editorial strengths, the prototype puts your design on parade. Remember, design is one of the main qualities that separates magazines from other media. They are far more eye-catching than newspapers and books and could take on a Web page any day of the week. To this end, there are two primary areas where the design is key.

Your Logo

Your logo, or nameplate, is your trademark. It must be distinctive and stand out from the rest. Also, it should be difficult or impossible to reproduce by a few simple strokes of the keyboard. You can't just have a 72-point Helvetica logo. Even to the design ignorant, it will look like you gave no effort to your magazine. And readers won't pick it up.

Your logo should be able to stand alone, regardless of what surrounds it. It should be an independent element that retains its beauty regardless of what pictures, colors, or words are around it.

Finally (and this may never have occurred to you), your logo needs to be one that can be reproduced easily on letterhead, business cards, T-shirts, baseball hats, and coffee mugs. If it involves eight different colors, fourteen shades of gray, and microscopic detail, then you're in big trouble. If it can't be reduced or enlarged with relative ease and clarity by a photocopier, then try again.

The Contents

Look at your table of contents. Make sure you have your magazine divided into three major sections (departments, columns, and features) and then be absolutely certain they follow proper design logic.

1. Departments

Departments are short and self-contained. Thus, they should be designed as such. They should be easily accessible and easily recognized. I'm not trying to insult the reader when I say this, but don't make the reader have to think about the design. It should not be confusing. Rather, it should make perfect, logical sense. Further, the departments should not compete with surrounding ads for sensationalistic design. Leave that to Madison Avenue art directors.

2. Columns

The columns should, of course, have the experts' names in plain view. However, you will probably want to include a picture as well. If he or she is famous, definitely include it. If the authority is not famous, but is relatively attractive or otherwise distinctive, and you feel the mug adds depth and humanity to the piece, include it if you like. Whatever the case, draw attention to both the writer and the subject matter with your column design.

3. Features

Here's where you let your creativity run wild. Because you're not locked into a single design theme as the departments and columns are, use your features to illustrate the depth of talent in your art department. The main thing to remember is that your editors and designers need to work

The main thing to remember is that your editors and designers need to work together to create a package guided by the premise that readers are looking for more information in less space and in less time.

together to create a package guided by the premise that readers are looking for more information in less space and in less time. So don't take a 1,500-word story and stretch it over twelve pages. Keep the design concise and clear. Anybody can blow up a picture to cover two pages, but that doesn't make it right.

Also, think horizontally when constructing your features. They should not be designed page to page, but rather from spread to spread. Create story layouts two pages at a time. The main reason for this is that an open magazine is roughly equal to your field of vision. Every time you turn the page, you are capable of seeing a single unit of design stretching from the left edge of one page to the right edge of the next. There is no sense in breaking up the natural inclination to take in these two pages at once.

Three Postulates of Design

As you plow through the design of the magazine, there are three major points about page layout that should be foremost in your mind. They hold true in every case, and provide a solid foundation for every design and redesign you will spearhead.

1. Inside Out

Start every spread design from the inside of the page and work your way to the edges. That way, you avoid the cardinal sin of graphic design—trapped white space. If you work from the outside in, you'll end up with unused space scattered randomly over the vital innards of the spread. It's a waste of space that clutters the layout. However, if you start from the middle and work toward the edges, you push white space to the outside. This way, the reader's eyes don't have to jump around the spread to get to the meat. It's centralized and concise.

2. One Focal Point

Your spread should have one and only one focal point per spread. Every layout should have a single, dominant element to which the eye is drawn first. If you have many elements of similar visual weight, the readers won't know where to begin or what to look at, and they'll likely turn the page. So give them a logical progression of images and text. Give them an entry point, then lead them through the spread with elements of descending visual weight.

3. Group the Pictures

Much like providing only one focal point, you need to arrange your pictures such that the reader doesn't have to jump all over the spread to take them all in. Group them. Put them close together so the reader can compare and contrast them. This way, it's far easier to make a point about what's in the photographs.

Gibberish

Don't sweat it concerning editorial copy for the prototype. All the features, columns, and departments can be gibberish. In fact, there are shareware computer programs available that will generate an endless amount of pseudo-Latin copy for such an occasion. The only copy that needs to be actual English and needs to match the content is the letter from the editor, the table of contents, the photo captions, the titles, and maybe the first paragraph of each story. Also, all photographs should be appropriate to their respective stories.

Advertisements

The inclusion of advertisements in your prototype can be tricky. Yes, it is easy to copy ads from existing magazines and insert them in your prototype and on your wish list, but beware. Even though this won't be circulated on newsstands, and even though nobody is paying for the ad, you could still be violating a copyright. Thus, you need to call the ad agency that produced the page and ask permission. It sounds crazy, but you'll wish you had done it when the agency's lawyer gives you a threatening phone call.

DON'T RUSH THE PROTOTYPE

In the end, remember that this is only a prototype. It is an authentic sample of what your magazine will be. You are under no particular deadline pressures and you don't have to deal with freelance writers. Therefore, take advantage of the opportunity to make a good impression. Don't rush it. By the time your magazine actually launches, you won't have the time or energy to dedicate to revamping dozens of flaws. So do it now while the pressure is off.

I said now.

David Getson is editorial director and publisher of Icon Thoughtstyle, *published by Icon L.P., in New York.* Icon, *a magazine for intelligent, ambitious young men, examines success and achievement in their most extreme manifestations. It was launched in 1997.*

Interview:

David Getson
Icon Thoughtstyle

When did you first formulate the *Icon* concept?

As a senior in college in 1993 at Princeton, like most people that age, I didn't know what I wanted to do. So that's where I was.

I started researching the lives of men who looked to me like they were successful. The scarcity of material and the scarcity of *good* material and the kind of information that I was looking for made me realize that there was something missing for someone in my position. I was reading biographies, autobiographies, watching documentaries, reading profiles, just to see how men took the steps to become successes in their fields. I began to realize that there could be one source of information that pooled that type of information.

So I started thinking about that. And it was actually when I read a profile of Hugh Hefner and how he started *Playboy* that it hit me that I could actually turn my interest of how people become successful into a magazine.

How did you recruit investors?

In the spring of 1994, I told an alumnus about my plan to make a magazine that helped young guys figure out where they could go with their lives, and he said, "Consider yourself to have your first investor." I turned him down at that point and told him that I was not ready for investors yet because I did not understand all of the elements that go into businesses. Although I had a pretty good idea for the concept of the magazine, I wanted to wait until I was better organized structurally.

I did take his investment a year later. He was my first investor. And along the way and in between, I went on a very intense search for all the knowledge that I would need to launch a magazine and to construct a business that could launch a magazine successfully. These are two different things. There is the concept and the idea for the magazine and philosophy and the vision, and then there is a very empirical and scientific business-oriented machinery that publishes that concept. I think that is where most entrepreneurial magazine publishers fail—in balancing the two of those. You either spot that niche and you try to create a machine that publishes for that niche or you have an idea for a philosophy or vision and you don't really care much about the machinery and the publishing aspects of the business. I tried to balance the two, and I spent a year talking to as many people in the publishing industry as possible.

How did you stay afloat financially?

At this point, I was still in college. I first came up with the concept of *Icon* in the winter of 1993 and by the time I talked to that investor in March, I had already been to New York many times doing research. Now, when I graduated and I knew that this was what I was going to do, I gathered what I call my seed capital. And I got my seed capital from three resources. First, I sold my car—a 1985 Chevy Celebrity—not very much money. Second, I had been given prize money for top thesis in my major at Princeton, but it, too, wasn't that much money. Also, at the end of the year I was given a special grant from the president's office to try and publish that thesis. None of those were very much money, but I managed to pool together the three where it gave me enough to move to New York for some time and start out in New York City. I also emptied all life savings, which wasn't very much, but it was enough for me to live out of the living room of two of my friends' apartment in the city. So I lived out of their common room for very low rent. I ate very little good food, did nothing socially, borrowed a lot of money from friends, ate a lot of macaroni and cheese, white rice, and water.

How did you hold on to your dedication at this point?

Well, that's something that people ask me all the time, but at no point since I moved out here have I thought of it as dedication. It is what I am, and I am what it is, and there is no difference between life and work. I never considered myself working, and I never considered doing anything else.

Meanwhile, I was able to find some help. Some people in NYC heard what I was doing through friends and they came to me. I sat down with them and explained what I was working toward and I said, "If you like what I'm doing and you can work for free, then join me." I hired two people like that. Luckily, they were both like me. They weren't paying rent themselves, for whatever reasons, so it was fortunate.

How did you sell the "work for free" idea to staff?

Well, those were the first people that I had ever discussed working with me. By the time I got to that point, I had convinced a graphic designer in Philadelphia who was a friend of the family to develop some logos for free. So I had some visual material that I could show them and prove to them that someone was working on this project with me. I had a lawyer—again, a friend of the family— who had already agreed to work with me and delay all fees. I still haven't paid them for their work, and that was three years ago.

So I was able to point to my lawyer, my graphic designer, and some stuff that I had written, and they could see that I had committed myself totally to this. And I really think, even with all that, it still takes a little persuasiveness.

I also tried to do everything *right*. I was very, very, very up front throughout the whole process—anytime I ever tried to recruit anyone or tried to do business with someone. I've never once tried to make what I've been doing into something bigger than what it was. So they could tell that I'd been up front and honest. There was no type of trickery going on. It was very clear. It was up to them. I told them about the risk that they would be taking and said, "Here's the potential, here's the upside, this is what I'm aiming for—there are no guarantees. If it's interesting, please join me." It was that kind of challenge and opportunity, and I guess that I was just lucky that I was able to find one or two people who were willing to try it.

Now, those two people who came on at the beginning, just to try it out, and just because they were warm bodies, are still here and both are key players. They both turned into amazingly talented professionals, even though none of us knew at the time that they were going to do so. I remember telling them both, "I don't care if you can't write a lick and you can't spell—I need *people*." And they are both great.

What advice would you give for recruiting staff?

Three things, probably. First, let them see how intensely you feel about the concept. Be able to explain it articulately, eloquently, with intensity and passion behind it.

That's one, but, second, it has to be balanced with honesty and awareness so they know that they are being led by someone who fully knows where the pitfalls are and who never tries to fool them into thinking that it's going to be easy. Instead, lay forth all the challenges, detours, and obstacles as clearly as possible so they'll know what they are getting into. That will inspire trust.

The third thing is to have as much material as you can, visually and verbally, about your concept. You have to show people that you have already done more work than they would ever have dreamed of. Show that you've done research and spent time shaping the concept—that kind of thing. Those are the three things that I would say.

After all of this, if they like the idea, then there should be no reason why they wouldn't give it a chance. My employees knew that any time that I was able to pay them, I would, and I would pay them more than I would take. They knew that.

You have your staff and you're living on nothing. Then what?

We then started developing the philosophy behind the magazine. We began describing the sections of the magazine, making sure every inch of it made sense in terms of its mission. I know that's something most new magazines—especially those started by young people with no experience—forget, and I know that there are a million of them. I had zero journalism experience. I had never written for a college newspaper, never had anything published or been in any way related to journalism.

But I learned from watching what Hefner did with *Playboy* that a magazine needs critical elements to be successful, and one of those is context and presentation.

Look at what Hefner did. He took sex and put it in an environment where guys would feel comfortable accessing what they really wanted. At the time, no one was doing that because of the context. There were magazines that just presented sex, but not in the right context. So I was thinking that with *Icon*, I wanted to do the same thing with ambition and success. I wanted guys to dream about their future, feel inspired about their chances, but not have it be a magazine about that. I wanted it to be contextually correct so men would feel comfortable accessing it.

I learned the other critical element from studying the industry, by talking to people, looking at the past, reading books about magazine history, and looking at current activity. I would look at magazines like *People Weekly* and the *Economist*—two magazines that I think are brilliantly edited and conceived.

One thing that strikes me about those magazines is that they never forget the metaphysics of the magazines. That is, they know what they are about and they do nothing else but that. They have a very consistent focus and are very aware of why people come to their magazines.

So during this time with these two people, I was writing philosophical discussions about the magazine. We would develop these discussions about the sections of the magazine while being very careful to keep them in line with the mission.

Meanwhile, we all were researching the industry and studying what other magazines did. We were learning from other magazines' successes and failures. Also, at that time, I was talking to as many people as possible in the industry. I actually just went through the list the other day and it kind of blows my mind. I was able to sit down with some of the leading publishing experts in journalism and on the business side of contemporary publishing and tell them my idea and let them grill it. And I listened to what they said. And believe me, everyone I talked to said, "You are going to fail." Everyone said, "Don't do it." And everyone said, "You stand a slim chance." That's fine. I understood immediately that that was going to be the first thing everyone said. I was warned a million times by everyone that it was going to fail, and it still very well could. Everyone knows the high chance of failure for a new consumer magazine.

Knowing that, what made you go ahead?

Because, to me, anytime someone said that I didn't have a chance or that I was going to fail, I kept thinking, "Well, of course, it's possible to launch a magazine successfully. It's been done before so that means that there's a way. And if there's a way, then I'm confident that I will find out the way."

So when people say that you can't do it, it just means that most people fail. It also struck me, when looking at the industry, that the reason why there is such a high failure rate is because it is so easy to create what looks like a magazine. Words and pictures on a page, to many people, is a magazine. It's not that hard to put words and pictures together. It is hard, very hard, to launch a business. A pharmaceutical business, a biotech business, or a magazine—it's all the same thing. It's still launching a business.

And that struck me early on because it *seemed* like an easy field to get into. You don't need to understand widgets and gadgets or anything like that. It made me think that maybe *that* was why there was such a high failure rate. It made me think that maybe, if I paid attention to the fact that it is a magazine on one hand and a business on the other, *I* would have a chance.

It also seemed pretty clear to me that there was a market. There seemed to be evidence. There was actually a lucrative and big market for what I was in. By that I mean a men's category. At the time there was only *GQ, Esquire,* and *Details*, really. *Men's Journal* and *Men's Health* were kind of new at that point, certainly not the big boys that they are now—at least in my mind, as a college student. What I saw, really, when it came down to it, was *GQ* and *Details* and nothing between them. That was high-fashion-conscious on one hand and downtown grungy on the other hand and nothing in between for ambitious young men. Now, the men's market has been saturated, it seems. But the niche I'm looking at is wide open, and that's for someone who is a little bit more intelligent and self confident and doesn't need a magazine to be his guide.

But here's the thing—every time a new competitor jumped into the market, it forced us to change a little bit. That's something that I guess is important. You start out with this idea and it changes, sometimes in big ways and sometimes in tiny ways, but they are all important because the key is to be different from anything else that is out there. We were always committed to putting out something that was different and better than anything else on the market on every level. So even though competitors came out, our commitment was still to make something different and that's something that we've been doing for two years.

Meanwhile, I was having to pay these people—not at that point, but after I took in my first investor, which was a year into it. I started to pay, and I have not missed payroll since. Those were some tough times and sometimes I would have to.... At one point, I was at a bar and drank sixteen ounces of maple syrup on a dare and got three hundred dollars for it and was able to meet payroll the next day. I ended up throwing up. I also got cash advances on my credit cards and ended up with about ten of those. I'm still paying off those credit card bills.

At that point, we knew we were putting together a prototype. So I knew that I wanted an art director in-house. I wanted someone that I could work with very closely to get the look and feel of the magazine. That was extremely important, at least to me. I was having this company in

Philadelphia develop logos for me for free, and I was learning very quickly that people who did stuff for free are not going to do it extremely passionately for very long.

And I was learning that I did not want *not* to pay people. This was a real business lesson because the first instinct is to try to get everyone you can to do everything they can for free. I no longer think that is a good philosophy. I think that it's better to pay. And I wanted the person who would do my design work to be paid.

So I went on a search for an art director and it was really our first big coup—to convince an internationally acclaimed art director who does work for two major magazines to take on *Icon* as a project. He started to develop pages and the people that I was working with started to see it turn from a concept into a project. It was very, very encouraging. It was also encouraging that someone with true experience in the field was willing to take a chance on *Icon*.

It also encouraged us that, along the way, all these publishing executives and journalists and editors that I had been talking to for advice were becoming a support network that backed us up and supported us. They gave my employees confidence that I knew what I was doing and that we were on the right path. And then we got our first profile. A subject agreed to do it. Hugh Hefner, the very man.

How did you pull that off?

I had my art director run a sample spread of what it would look like, and I wrote a full-page letter describing how his story inspired me to start this company and this magazine. I told him I wanted to bring that story to as many people as possible. That's exactly what I am trying to do with this magazine, and he agreed. That was something that gave us all the little jolt of encouragement that we were on the right path. Meanwhile, I started to get a couple of investors here and there, and we were starting to gain some momentum as a business.

At that point, as we started to work on the prototype, the art director pulled out and left us. Many things went wrong, but my art director bailing out on us was one of the biggest things that we had to deal with. It turned out to be one of the best things that could have happened to *Icon*. I went on a search for a new art director. At that point, I was talking to one of the vice presidents of design at Warner Brothers. He was one of the people we had become friendly with, so he gave us a list of people.

I interviewed all of them, and they were all willing to do it. But the guy at the bottom of the list, the one who had no experience, was the one.

We all immediately saw the chemistry, but I also saw that his designs were not right for the magazine. I had him design a logo as a sample and it was all wrong. Over the course of a couple of weeks, I asked him to design a spread, and it, too, was all wrong. One day we sat down for about three or four hours, and I brought out every book and magazine that I had stored up with me and used them as an example of what I was looking for. I told him what we needed at *Icon* and why we felt he would be the right guy even though I had not seen it from him yet. I told him what we had to do. He said he could do it, and, since then, he has totally done it.

He was also able to elucidate some of the things about the magazine which we had been unable to elucidate until then—just during the course of the conversation. By doing that, it became clear to me that he was in the right frame of mind because he realized that this magazine has a very distinctive set of philosophies. And I just felt that he, better than anyone else, was able to reach that.

I strongly believe that, in order to succeed, we have to stay strictly within the lines of our philosophy, and I have to be certain that everyone here also thinks that way. Some aspect or mission of the philosophy has been the source of many fights. When I have failed to communicate all aspects of the mission, some of the new people that work here have tried to do something that is not within the perimeter of our world. They take offense or they don't understand. And that will result in conflict. We have actually had people come and go, quit, or be fired because I failed to enable them to understand why something was inconsistent with our philosophy. But I know 100% within my heart that if you waiver from that philosophy, you are risking failure. And if you stick to that philosophy, even though some people may think that it's a bad idea, you're crazy, or whatever, at least you have a chance.

We have to be devout. We have to be fanatic about keeping everything within our magazine's mission and personality. That was something that I knew instinctively.

Now, none of what I say and what I think has been proven successful. That is something that I want to make absolutely clear. I put out one issue of that magazine. By no means does that mean anything at all. Anyone can put out one issue of a magazine. This is something that I think is important for someone launching a magazine to agree with and believe because launching a magazine is nothing. It's being around for a year. It's achieving what you set out to do. Lots of people can put out one issue. But I don't know if it's going to work or not; I'm just telling you what my instincts are.

The next thing I did was build an editorial committee. Robin, the first employee, and I conceived the committee. It was for our service section, "Iconnoisseur." We wanted to gain credibility with our readers, and also some credibility with our investors. We created a body called the Iconnoisseur Experts Committee, and this actually turned out to be a big step for us. Robin successfully solicited the help of about a dozen or so experts from several areas of the field. So we got about two or three people per field to sit officially on our unpaid editorial board of watchdogs that, basically, would be our *Good Housekeeping* Seal of Approval for that section. It would basically prove that any piece we published lived up to these expert standards.

That turned into a good selling point with our investors. It's like their name is on our masthead. It's a selling point with advertisers, and it's also a good watchdog and a good critical entity that makes sure our material is good. And that took a while. That was something that took my art director's help in creating invitations and constitutions. We sent out many mailings, and it was a long process, but we got about a 90% acceptance rate. So that was very good.

At that point, I had raised a sizable amount of money. But in order to do that—and here is the biggest, biggest thing I could ever say to anyone launching a magazine—I learned very early on that, no matter how good your concept is, if your business plan doesn't live up to and exceed the quality of your concept, then you will have a very slim chance of raising the money that the concept requires. That means that as much time and money that you spend on the concept, philosophy, and vision of the magazine, you will probably have to double in order to make a business plan that will support such a concept.

I'm saying this because I am someone who knocked on probably a million doors, literally, for individual investors to finance my concept, and I was laughed out of many offices. So I started to put together a business plan and had *that* laughed out of a million offices.

The first consultant I ever hired was to help develop my business plan, and we did that. During all the months that we have already talked about, I was doing that while we were working on the concept, and I was able to get my hands on existing business plans from the magazine industry. I met enough people so that one or two had access to business plans. They probably shouldn't have given them to me, but I was able to look at them, study them, and take what was useful to me. When I look back at my original business plans, they are funny. They are embarrassing, but when you are 21 or 22 years old and you have the business plan that I had, people at least start to listen to you and take you seriously and give you advice.

Eventually my business plan, in the words of media investment bankers in New York City, was one of the best business plans they had ever seen. We just got fanatical about that. We went overboard making the business plan airtight.

At this point I was developing the business plan, and it was decent. The other thing is that when the business plan was decent, I dressed it up visually. I bound it, and I had my art director help me with it. It might be the most cynical statement in the world, but that helped me to present it. It might not have been the best business plan in the world, but it helped me present the business plan appeal because it looked good and people were more receptive to it than when I just stapled it together.

Also at that point, I was able to move. With three people in the company and a decent business plan, I had raised enough private money that I was able to move offices to where we are now. Then I recruited this guy from Solomon Brothers and we built a great business plan, and I was able to raise a significant amount of money.

I was also able to create the prototype, which is the second thing that I would tell someone about to start a magazine. Develop a prototype and basically publish it to the industry. It worked for us, that much I can say. We created a live prototype. I think it was about seventy pages, perfect bound, professionally produced, and printed at a press run of about 5,000.

We used live editorial and original photography. Most prototypes are about ten pages, in Greek text with stock photography. It may have an original cover and that's it. We were in a position where we could do everything overboard. At least that was my belief, and we created this selling tool for advertisers, investors, and the media.

Before we did that, I had my art director create two or three hand-bound prototypes for investor usage. With that hand-bound prototype, I was able to hire my advertising director as well. Again, I point out that recruiting an advertising director with experience was another huge move for us because, as a start-up, you are facing a huge mountain. You have to compete against the big boys in filling up ad space, which is particularly tough, especially when you are starting out with a small circulation.

Everyone is skeptical of start-ups and no one has money or time to waste, so if we didn't have an art director with experience and contacts, I don't know what would have happened to us. But because we had a beautiful prototype we were able to recruit our advertising director. At that point we had three of them. We taped them up, hand-bound them, sprayed color laser prints on cardboard, and stapled them and taped them together.

Once we got our advertising director, we started to make our official prototype. Here's what we did with our prototype, and again this is just a strategy. We "sold" advertising space into our prototype based on our advertising director's contacts. We were able to get some meetings with people, tell them what we wanted to do, show them the hand-bound prototype, tell them we were creating a prototype, and tell them that if they would cover costs of production, they would have free space in the prototype.

That went great. We sent one to everyone we could think of. Then we started to get press and attention from people, and we were even able to raise more money at that point. And that was just a little while ago. Time has flown by so quickly that I have trouble remembering. But the prototype and the media kit that we created to house the prototype were serious financial projects and serious, major projects that made my team learn how to work together and learn what it takes to create a magazine—both on the advertising side and the editorial side. We hired a couple of more people, and all along, at every step of the way, I was constantly raising money.

How did you target investors?

It's not like there is an organized network of these individuals, but in any town and in every city and borough of America there are high net-worth individuals who will invest in private ventures, and some of them know each other and some of them don't. It's just a lot of pounding the pavement and a lot of persistence for a person to expand their pool of contacts. Every time you meet someone, you ask if he knows someone. Ask if he feels comfortable making an introduction, and you never stop following up.

So we sent business plans and materials to potential investors around the country and around the world—and we're talking about hundreds and hundreds. And a handful of them said yes, but it was enough to finance the magazine.

And here is the next bullet point, the next major thing that I would recommend to anyone starting a magazine. That is: Learn to love the pain of disappointment and failure.

What I mean is, if you don't understand that, rejection and failure will come at every step of the way.

About a year-and-a-half ago, I learned to assume that if I wanted something from someone and he said no, it's his *job* to say no. But it's *my* job, first off, to assume that he will say no. Then, I have to make sure that I successfully convey to him what we are all about. It's my job to help him understand why he should say yes. No is not an insult or rejection; it means that he hasn't gotten all of the information he needs. That's the way I always think of it. There is no reason why anyone should say no to me except for the fact that I haven't communicated what an opportunity I am presenting.

So anytime someone says no, then great, it gives me an opportunity to figure out why I wasn't effective in communicating something. You have to really use it as an opportunity. If someone says no, I don't just say, "OK, thank you, good-bye." I say, "OK, can I take a moment to ask you why you feel that way? I'm not surprised that you said that. I would say no, too, unless I saw this, so let me send you fill-in-the-blank." It's never, "OK, fine good-bye," unless they really, really mean no, which does sometimes happen once in a while and that's just the way that it is.

But because every step of the way presents a million failures and rejections and detours, if you don't learn to see that, then you get discouraged rather quickly. And in order to raise the money that we raised, I first had to be rejected by more people than I care to remember or count. It's the same with advertising.

Talk about the name *Icon*.

The word *icon* means a religious symbol of worship, like a religious icon or crucifix. Basically, a symbol that people have accepted and bow down to. The magazine is an ironic use of the word. We don't believe in icons in that way, but in worshipping and referring to the symbol, and in understanding its origins, we either accept it or reject it. But never worship it. Any icon.

This magazine is about icons of success. Men who have successfully taken steps, and through their actions have become symbols or exaggerations—simplifications of themselves. And we are trying to show the reader that they are not these simplified symbols, but rather are actual human beings that did X, Y, and Z and became icons. The thought is that by humanizing these people, our readers will realize that they can do anything they want to do. They can simply make enormous accomplishments. That's why I use that name.

What about the actual launch?

The next thing for us was a relentless commitment to the highest quality that we could achieve. That means both with the writers and with the photographers, and that also means with advertisers.

What you see in issue 1 are twenty-two pages of the top advertisers in the men's category. Production-wise, as well, we are pouring a lot of money into creating a good quality magazine, and it's yet to be seen whether or not the market will sustain that quality. I don't know if the demand will be there, but that's what we've set out to do. If you look at the paper quality, the binding, the texture and the quality of the photos, you will see, hopefully, that this is a superior quality product. That might be a mistake, I don't know.

How were you able to sell people on the first issue?

Advertising is and was a major challenge, and, again, it's a numbers game. We see so many accounts and so many people at those accounts, that we're bound to get a handful if our target hits their target. You have to be flexible. We offer very low rates and do have charter advertising deals. These are designed especially for early adopters, as we like to call them.

My main goal as publisher is to create a magazine that is able to handle not just lifestyle advertising, but also career-oriented advertising. That means lifestyle and career, such as financial, computer, and credit card. All of that right alongside high-end fashion and liquor ads. There's a lot of stuff there. You will see IBM, Gucci, Skyy Vodka, and Calvin Klein.

How do you get Calvin Klein in your magazine?

Well, first you have an advertising director who has spent twelve years in the fashion category. Next, you have a beautiful prototype. For fashion advertisers, yes, that extra is crucial. Next, you have a lot of press in the trade and in the fashion and retail media as well. For an advertiser like Calvin Klein—someone who is really known for heading trends, not following them—you really have a chance if you offer them a good deal. Calvin Klein doesn't follow people; he leads people. So it makes sense for people to take a chance on him because Calvin Klein is a pioneer.

It was also very difficult to get any advertising from the Detroit area and the auto category. Anyone who is launching a magazine should know that if you don't have someone in the Detroit area, your chances are slim to none that you are going to get advertising from Detroit. So we have representatives in Detroit and we have representatives on the West Coast as well. We are very streamlined here. We're understaffed. In NYC, three or four people might be able to handle it, but you are certainly stretching it. They are not going to be able to handle the West Coast as well. That's been major for us. We were able to pull in two auto ads, which was very rare for a start-up.

The other thing is our relationship with the press. One of the reasons why we have been able to launch the way we have is because we have been a fixture in New York media for about a year now. Anytime the men's category has been mentioned, *Icon* has been named. And that has not been by chance. That was very conscious and deliberate on our part.

What I did was delegate that realm of activity to a person here on staff. One of the things that person did was act as a liaison between the media and *Icon*, and basically inundate them with information.

My art director would design stuff specifically for the press, which enabled us to form a very specific relationship with them. I think that is very important because you want to be able to let people know what you are doing. Our advertisers have been hearing about us, and they say "Wow, your PR people are really doing a good job." We didn't even *have* PR people.

We also sent out a series of postcards as part of our PR effort. We had some stuff on the front, and on the back we had a quote that said, "No men's magazine focusing in on substantive issues has ever succeeded." That was a quote from a very big advertising person here in New York City who said that about *Icon* in a trade article. It was the first piece ever written about us.

We turned that into a PR opportunity. We plastered that on the back of thousands of postcards and sent them out around the country. And we said, "Coming soon, the response." And a couple of weeks later, we sent another postcard with a sample cover and an answer that said, basically, "Look, yeah, it's true, and we think we know why, and watch out because here it comes." That generated a little bit of interest, and we were able to get some press. But now I have a PR firm, and they're very good.

Was this contracted out?

Yes. That's a good point because we have contracted out a couple of key positions around here. I think that with a start-up, unless you have so much money that you are just swimming in it, then you will have to outsource a number of different things. Our production staff is outsourced, our circulation staff is outsourced, and some of our advertising representatives are outsourced. It's a key strategy, I guess, for any start-up.

NOTES

. . . .

. . . .

. . . .

. . . .

. . . .

. . . .

. . . .

. . . .

. . . .

. . . .

. . . .

. . . .

. . . .

. . . .

. . . .

. . . .

. . . .

The media kit may be inappropriately named. It should be called the "hype kit." With it, you'll be attempting to generate discussion about your forthcoming publication in every nook and cranny of the advertising community. And where there's discussion, there are returned phone calls and client lunches.

THE MEDIA KIT 14

If you blush at the mention of shameless self-promotion, you're in the wrong business. At the very least, you're reading the wrong chapter. The media kit is all about the "essence of me." In a nutshell, the media kit provides advertising executives with every shred of information about your publication they will need in order to place an ad on behalf of their clients.

THE MAJOR ROLE

Advertising account executives are the gatekeepers of the advertising dollars. Without their approval, you're sunk. Thus, the media kit's major role is to introduce them to your concept and educate them about the nature of your magazine and your strategy.

Tell them how you will serve their needs and the needs of their clients. These ad executives and media buyers are always looking for new outlets to reach a specific audience. If that outlet is you, scream it from the mountaintop. Give them a comprehensive look at how your magazine will be different from the competition. Tell them how your magazine will offer a brand-spanking-new vehicle for nailing this audience.

The Contents

In the space of five to eight pages, you'll be laying out the main points from your business plan. Although you won't divulge the secrets of your four-year budget, you will get into the nitty-gritty of everything else.

The Mission Statement

It may help, for dramatic effect, to lay your mission statement out on a page all by itself. Make sure every word counts. Because this will be the first page the ad execs see, you want to whet appetites, not bore to tears. Leave them wanting to know more.

Audience Analysis

Again, the point of the media kit is education. Ad execs may know the audience they want to reach like the back of their hands, but you may have found a better one. Or, your research may have uncovered some tasty morsels they weren't aware of. For your magazine, *Collectible Band-Aids*, you might have unearthed the fact that every single Band-Aid collector in America prefers the Beatles to the Rolling Stones. Any advertising exec worth his salt would like to know this.

Because more and more ad execs are getting their MBAs, gear your media kit toward someone with a head for numbers and a heart for making a buck.

So, on a single sheet, hit the high points of your demographic and psychographic research. Because more and more ad execs are getting their MBAs, gear your media kit toward someone with a head for numbers and a heart for making a buck.

Competition Analysis

Don't go overboard here. Ad execs know who your competition is, and they know exactly what your competitors have to offer. Thus, the point here is to set yourself apart. Don't do this by insulting the other magazines. If you go off on some wild rant about your competition's evil publishing empire and their plot to kill your family, you'll throw your credibility out the window. Keep it professional and upbeat. Remember, this is about *you*.

Circulation Breakdown

Get straight to the point with circulation. No need to write a novel about every newsstand in America you hope to be on. Simply tell the ad exec who your distributor is and what your overall philosophy is. *Icon Thoughtstyle Magazine* begins its circulation analysis by saying, "Icon has developed a highly targeted distribution plan that stresses efficiency and exposure. Initial distribution will focus on the top twenty domestic and international markets in addition to a strong effort in major bookstores and other outlets where *Icon* believes it will have access to its readers."

From there, hit the high points from your business plan— how many you'll print, your projected ratio of single-copy to direct mail sales, whether your circulation will be audited, and so forth.

The Rate Card

Your advertising rate card is a fairly no-frills element, but it's the bottom line for the ad execs. They have a budget to work with, and you'd like to squeeze into it. In as clear a chart as possible, break down the cost of your ads—from black and white up to full color, from a quarter-page to a full-page, from one issue to a three-year contract. Clarity is key.

Editorial Calendar

If you haven't done this yet, now would be a good time. You need to let the ad agencies know what you're up to. Give them a schedule of upcoming editorial content so they'll have a better idea of what to expect. If your magazine, *Highways and Byways*, will contain six consecutive cover stories on gruesome interstate wrecks, most ad executives will want to steer clear. Unless their clients happen to be airbag manufacturers.

Also in this section, give the ad agencies the deadlines for each issue and the dates each issue will hit newsstands. Finally, give them the dimensions and a general physical description of your magazine. They can't design an ad if they don't know what size to make it.

The Prototype

Let's put this baby to good use—include a copy of the prototype in every media kit. Ad execs need to see that all of the business plan elements actually do come together to form a magazine their market would read.

If you cannot squeeze the expense of printing a prototype into your prelaunch budget, then include a few pages of sample designs. Give them a department spread or a feature layout. Also, throw in a couple of cover designs. Even if they don't have a formal prototype in their hands, they can still get a handle on what you're trying to accomplish design-wise.

Who Gets It

All dressed up and no place to go? Once you've got a tip-top media kit, you'll need to know where to send it. Do not mail it to the businesses you want to advertise. Send it to the ad agency that represents them.

Your two sources for this information are at your local library (assuming it's a big one). Every six months, two big, red books called the *National Directory Advertisers* and the *National Directory of Advertising Agencies* are published. In them, you'll find everything you need to know concerning who advertises where, which agency represents them, and which advertising executive works their account. It's the final word on where to go for media kit mailing addresses.

THE PRESS KIT

You need to educate and excite more than just the advertising agencies. Stroking the media couldn't hurt, either. Enter the press kit.

The press kit, technically speaking, is the media kit minus the advertising rate card. The goal is to educate the media outlets rather than the media buyers. In the name of hype, you should try to convince them that you're the Next Big Thing in the magazine industry.

The ultimate goal here is to make your magazine a house-hold term before it even hits newsstands. Try to get inter-viewed on television or in newspapers. This is what America is all about. Heck, NBC's logo is a peacock! Does that tell you anything?

The Envelope

Just like the direct mail pieces, you've got to package your media kit in an envelope and folder that screams, "Open Me!" Don't think for one minute that these ad executives aren't swarmed every day by people just like you. Their desks are piled high with promotional materials like yours. If you think your house is swamped with junk mail, try being the gateway to advertising dollars.

Thus, the more creative your presentation, the better. It must stand out from the stack. When *Lear's* launched, they put their media kit in an accordion-like envelope that looked like an attaché case. *Better Homes and Gardens* bound theirs in extra heavy-duty plastic folders. Though the success of your magazine does not rest solely in the creativity behind your media kit, you still need it to grab attention. Go as far as your budget permits.

The Follow-up

If you've budgeted a great deal of money for your media kit, there are some tricks you can hide up your sleeve. Try using a delivery service. Yes, it's expensive, but it will be opened first and the ad execs will know you think they're special.

If you have the time, try delivering the media kit in person. Where Fed Ex or UPS is nice, personal delivery is right up there with a dozen roses when it comes to special feelings.

Also, try calling the agencies about a week or two after they receive your package. Give them time to read it and discuss it around the office. Thank them for their attention and ask if they have any further questions. And, budget permitting, request a meeting. Personal contact is always the most effective way to get your point across.

> **If you think your house is swamped with junk mail, try being the gateway to advertising dollars.**

FINALLY

Remember, these people control a sizable chunk of your revenue. If you don't sway opinions in the advertising community, you're running a business with one hand tied behind your back. There's no sense in it. Hit them with a good media kit.

Let them know you plan to own the newsstand, and you intend to take them with you on your rise to the top.

It's only fair.

Carole Ference is founding publisher of Live! *magazine, which covers the world of entertainment outside the home.* Live! *was founded in 1996.*

Interview:

Carole Ference
Live!

Who came up with the concept for *Live!*?

It came from my boss, the CEO of TicketMaster, Fred Rosen.

How did you get involved in it?

I had been with the Hearst Corporation for eight and half years. Prior to that, I was publisher of *House Beautiful* magazine for three years. Before that, I was publisher of *Connoisseur* magazine for a year and a half, and before that I was associate publisher of *Town & Country*. I was with *Atlantic Monthly* as the New York manager before that, and I started with the *New York Times* in 1980.

So what attracted you to this project?

Really, the excitement of the business proposition and of the editorial. Number one, the editorial is unique. It is targeted to people who consume lots of live entertainment—who are really the most passionate entertainment fans—so the editorial is very targeted, very niched.

The business side of the proposition is incredibly compelling. To me, it represents the future of publishing. We not only have started a magazine which is very targeted to a very targeted audience, but we are owned by an entertainment company. This allows us to tap into all the entertainment assets that TicketMaster owns. That is what advertisers and marketers are looking for—that very integrated approach to reaching a certain target market in a number of different ways, in a number of forms of communication.

So we have the Web site, we have ticket backs, and ticket envelopes. We know exactly where that entertainment consumer is going to be at certain moments of time, so we can absolutely reach them with frequency and in a number of different ways. That is what got me excited about the proposition.

I guess with *Live!* there was not really a problem with recruiting investors.

No, because when I joined, it was owned privately by Fred Rosen and Paul Allen, who cofounded Microsoft with Bill Gates. So it was privately owned, but then it went public in November of 1996.

Is this the first magazine you have been with right from the launch?

Yes.

What were some of the problems you encountered?

I think we are so unique in the way we launched. We started out with almost five hundred thousand subscribers because Fred Rosen and TicketMaster tried it out for years with a very modest pamphlet called an *Entertainment Guide*. It was a listing of live events in your hometown. They had thirty-five different versions.

Through their fifteen telephone centers, they were selling a year's subscription to this very modest pamphlet, which had no advertising. It was just a pamphlet with the listings, and they were getting an average of twelve dollars for a year's subscription. Fred just thought, "Gee, think if we had a magazine with information these avid fans would love to know."

So we started out with a lot of subscribers, which is rare. We did not have to scramble for a base. We had it sort of built in. I think the challenge was going monthly with this huge audience. We could change because we had revenue from these people who were already subscribing to the guide. Then we converted them to *Live!* by binding the same guide into the new magazine. They were absolutely getting more for their money.

So the challenge there was to go monthly in the beginning—not only from the editorial side, but the business side—because most new magazines publish two to four times a year. There are not that many that go four times a year. So that was a big challenge from the editorial side. From the business side, in terms of all the aspects for fulfillment and advertising, we had to get up and running like a mature magazine of 500,000 readers within months and immediately go monthly. We had no time to work out any of the bugs.

What advice would you give for launching a magazine?

Be sure you are willing to stay in for the long term, before you are making money. And make sure you have enough money to get it through infancy to adolescence to adulthood.

It takes more money and time than you would ever imagine. You just have to be patient. You have to be prepared to invest money, to build money into the brand name. TicketMaster has a lot of visibility and a lot of equity, and that has helped us. But *Live!* magazine, as a single entity, is brand new. So you really have to spend the money and be sure you are on target strategically to build that equity.

Through the launch process, and especially at the very beginning, did you ever get discouraged?

Never. That is not my personality.

Do you think you have an undying dedication to make it?

It is missionary work. You have to have that missionary spirit and that belief, and you have to proselytize everybody. A lot of that is your belief and your fortitude and your enthusiasm for it.

The other part are the relationships that I've built over the years as a publisher and by being in this business. It's people saying, "Yes, I know Carol. She is good, she is smart, she is going to get involved with something that is going to work." A lot of it, from the advertising side especially, is about relationships. That keeps you going.

How many years did it take you to build these relationships?

Sixteen or seventeen years. I started selling at the *New York Times* corporate financial and some of those people are still running agencies, or are media directors, or whatever. As a publisher, you get in to see higher level people. So once you get a title, if you use it properly and you are smart about how you use it, and you get results for these people, it is easier to get to the higher-level people.

Were you involved with the hiring of the staff?

Absolutely. There was nothing here when we arrived.

What did you look for in staff members?

People who were experienced in magazine publishing, number one, and people who were hard working and creative, who I felt had that missionary spirit, who enjoy a good challenge, and who would be resilient not only with a new venture but also with the unknown. So I think those are the qualities.

But I think you have to be flexible because magazines are organic. So you have to be willing to fine tune it as you go along, without deviating from your vision and mission. That is, you have to supply this constituency in a clearly-defined way. With *Live!*, we give the entertainment customer what they want—what they want to read, what information they need—and then we're willing to fine tune it when we get feedback and conduct focus groups. So you have to make sure you are on the right track.

The end is nigh. Hopefully, you've followed the guidelines laid out in the last couple of hundred pages and are now resting this book on a stack of papers that resembles a business plan.

Let's run down all the elements you should have together for your business plan.

☐ The Concept

Write your mission statement, your guiding light, in no more than three sentences. In fact, if you can boil it down to one sentence, you're better off. Make it clear and concise, then memorize it like it's your own name.

☐ The Contents

Break your magazine's contents down into departments, columns, and features (don't forget the table of contents page and the letter from the editor). For the business plan, you'll need to drape four issues' worth of specific contents over this skeleton. Give the potential investor a couple of months' worth of ideas and stories so he'll have a better idea about what you're up to.

☐ Letter from the Editor

It may seem premature, but go ahead and write the letter from the editor for the premiere issue. Remember, explain your motives to the readers, and make them feel like the magazine belongs to them.

☐ Audience Analysis

Once you've done research on your audience, boil it down to demographics and psychographics. Lay it all out here for your potential investors and advertisers to chew on.

☐ Competition Analysis

Scan the newsstand, check the reference books, and list your competition. Dedicate one page per major competitor, providing their circulation, ad rate, concept, and, above all, the weaknesses upon which you will capitalize.

Then list your minor competitors, minus the individual weaknesses and without dedicating an entire page to each one. At the end of the list give a summary of the entire minor lot.

Once you've got all competitors enumerated and analyzed, write a two- or three-paragraph executive summary detailing what you've found. This page should lead off this section.

☐ Advertising Analysis

This is what we call the "wish list." Thumb through your competitors' publications and make a list of all the advertisers you'd like to steal from them. Then, add to the list all those advertisers they don't have but you want.

☐ Circulation Analysis

Remember how much circulation costs? Well, that's why this section is so crucial. In this part of your business plan, lay out your strategy for moving your magazine from the press to the people. It's more complex than it seems, and can be more expensive than it needs to be. Determine what percentage will go to single-copy sales, to direct mail, and to promotional freebies.

☐ Staff

Determine whom you will need and what you will pay them. Remember, employees can get expensive, but you're magazine (and your marriage) will sink if you understaff.

Find the balance.

☐ The Budget

This is the most time-consuming and complex element in your business plan. You've got to lay out all of your expenses and revenues for the next four years. Your investor may turn to this section first, so do it right. Make the bottom line clear for each fiscal period and, above all, be honest. You can't publish a magazine from prison.

☐ The Contingency Plan

It's the home stretch. Take all of the above elements and boil them down to a single page. Your potential investors don't want to have to read the entire business plan at first sight. Instead, give them the highlights from each section so they can get an idea of what you're doing in five minutes or less.

PUTTING IT TOGETHER

Once you've assembled each section of your business plan, once you've thought it all through, analyzed it, planned ahead, and prepared for the worst, put it all together in a well-organized folder or notebook.

Don't believe the old saying that you can't judge a book by its cover. If your business plan looks amateurish, your investor will think he's wasting his time on a lightweight, and he won't give you a dime. Give it a little design. You could even borrow the services of your soon-to-be graphic designer to give it a little pep.

GRAND FINALE

Now is the time put your words into action. As I mentioned more than once, magazine ideas come by the dozen and are worth a dime. It is the proper execution of the idea that will make a great magazine.So, without further delay, get out of your seat and launch the best new magazine ever published.

Good luck.

Index